The Voysey Inheritance

Harley Granville Barker (1877–1946) was the most
brilliant British director of the first quarter of the twentieth
century. His best known plays, including *Waste* (banned by the
Lord Chamberlain), were written as contributions to his
Company's repertoire of provocative modern drama for a
subsidised national theatre, a cause he championed in his book
A National Theatre: Scheme and Estimates. Waste was first presented
by the Stage Society, 1907, and revised and produced at the
Westminster Theatre, 1936. Other plays include *The Madras
House,* first produced at Duke of York's Theatre, 1910, revised
1925 for production at Ambassadors' Theatre; *The Secret Life*,
produced at the Orange Tree Theatre, Richmond, 1989, and
His Majesty, first produced at the Edinburgh International
Festival at St Bride's Centre by Orange Tree Theatre Company
in 1992.

Harley Granville Barker

The Voysey Inheritance

Methuen Drama

Published by Methuen 2006

1 3 5 7 9 10 8 6 4 2

Methuen Publishing Limited
11–12 Buckingham Gate
London SW1E 6LB

The play was first published in August 1909, revised edition March 1913,
further revised 1934 and published 1938 by Sidgwick & Jackson Ltd, London.
This edition contains the 1934 revised play.

Methuen Publishing Limited Reg. No. 3543167

A CIP catalogue record for this book is available from the British Library

ISBN 0 413 77609 3
978 0 413 77609 9

Typeset by Country Setting, Kingsdown, Kent
Printed and bound in Great Britain by
Bookmarque Ltd, Croydon, Surrey

The Voysey Inheritance premiered in its original version at the
Court Theatre, Sloane Square, London, on 7 November 1905,
with the following cast:

Mr Voysey	A.E. George
Mrs Voysey	Florence Haydon
Trenchard Voysey, KC	Eugene Mayeur
Major Booth Voysey	Charles Fulton
Edward Voysey	Thalberg Corbett
Hugh Voysey	Dennis Eadie
Honor Voysey	Geraldine Olliffe
Ethel Voysey	Alexandra Carlisle
Mrs Hugh Voysey (Beatrice)	Henrietta Watson
Mrs Booth Voysey (Emily)	Miss Grace Edwin
Denis Tregoning	Frederick Lloyd
Alice Maitland	Mabel Hackney
Mr George Booth	O.B. Clarence
Rev. Evan Colpus	Edmund Gwenn
Peacey	Trevor Lowe
Phoebe	Gwynneth Galton
Mary	Mrs Fordyce
Christopher	Harry C. Duff

The play was revived at the Shaftesbury Theatre, London, in a revised version of the text (that of the present edition) on 25 May 1934, with the following cast:

Mr Voysey	Felix Aylmer
Mrs Voysey	May Whitty
Trenchard Voysey, KC	Harcourt Williams
Major Booth Voysey	Archibald Batty
Edward Voysey	Maurice Evans
Hugh Voysey	Marius Goring
Honor Voysey	Antonia Brough
Ethel Voysey	Hermione Hannen
Mrs Hugh Voysey (Beatrice)	Joyce Bland
Mrs Booth Voysey (Emily)	Joan Harben
Denis Tregoning	Ernest Hare
Alice Maitland	Beatrix Thomson
Mr George Booth	O.B. Clarence
Rev. Evan Colpus	George Devine
Peacey	Frank Napier
Phoebe	Joan Leister
Mary	Freda Silcock
Christopher	Horace McBane

Directed by the author and Harcourt Williams

The play was revived in the Lyttelton auditorium of the
Royal National Theatre, London, on 18 April 2006, with the
following cast:

Mr Voysey	Julian Glover
Mrs Voysey	Doreen Mantle
Trenchard Voysey, KC	Mark Tandy
Major Booth Voysey	Andrew Woodall
Edward Voysey	Dominic West
Hugh Voysey	Martin Hutson
Honor Voysey	Lucy Briers
Ethel Voysey	Isabella Calthorpe
Mrs Hugh Voysey (**Beatrice**)	Kirsty Bushell
Mrs Booth Voysey (**Emily**)	Sarah Mowat
Denis Tregoning	Joseph Thompson
Alice Maitland	Nancy Carroll
Mr George Booth	John Nettleton
Rev. Evan Colpus	Roger Swaine
Peacey	John Normington
Phoebe	Julia West
Mary	Anna Steel
Company	David Baron
Company	Christopher Gilling
Company	Max Dowler
Company	Sinead O'Keeffe

Directed by Peter Gill
Designed by Alison Chitty
Lighting by Hartley T.A. Kemp
Music by Terry Davies

The Voysey Inheritance

The action of the play takes place in the office of Voysey and Son in Lincoln's Inn and in the dining room of Mr Voysey's house in Chislehurst.

In accordance with Granville Barker's practice, emphasised words and phrases in dialogue are indicated by spaced rather than italic type (e.g., e m p h a s i s e d , not *emphasised*).

Act One

The Office of Voysey and Son is in the best part of Lincoln's Inn. Its panelled rooms give out a sense of grandmotherly comfort and security, very grateful at first to the hesitating investor, the dubious litigant. **Mr Voysey***'s own room, into which he walks about twenty past ten of a morning, radiates enterprise besides. There is polish on everything; on the windows, on the mahogany of the tidily packed writing-table that stands between them, on the brasswork of the fireplace in the other wall, on the glass of the firescreen which preserves only the pleasantness of a sparkling fire, even on* **Mr Voysey***'s hat as he takes it off to place it on the little red-curtained shelf behind the door.* **Mr Voysey** *is sixty or more and masterful; would obviously be master anywhere from his own home outwards, or wreck the situation in his attempt. Indeed there is sometimes a buccaneering air in the twist of his glance, not altogether suitable to a family solicitor. On this bright October morning,* **Peacey***, the head clerk, follows just too late to help him off with his coat, but in time to take it and hang it up with a quite unnecessary subservience. Relieved of his coat,* **Mr Voysey** *carries to his table the bunch of beautiful roses he is accustomed to bring to the office three times a week and places them for a moment only near the bowl of water there ready to receive them while he takes up his letters. These lie ready too, opened mostly, one or two private ones left closed and discreetly separate. By this time the usual salutations have passed, Peacey's 'Good morning, sir';* **Mr Voysey***'s 'Morning, Peacey'. Then as he gets to his letters* **Mr Voysey** *starts his day's work.*

Mr Voysey   Any news for me?

Peacey   I hear bad accounts of Alguazils Preferred, sir.

Mr Voysey   Oh . . . who from?

Peacey   Merrit and James's head clerk in the train this morning.

Mr Voysey   They looked all right on . . . Give me *The Times*.

Peacey *goes to the fireplace for* The Times; *it is warming there.* **Mr Voysey** *waves a letter, then places it on the table.*

Mr Voysey   Here, that's for you . . . Gerrard's Cross business. Anything else?

Peacey (*as he turns* The Times *to its finance page*)   I've made the usual notes.

Mr Voysey   Thank'ee.

Peacey   Young Benham isn't back yet.

Mr Voysey   Mr Edward must do as he thinks fit about that. Alguazils, Alg – oh, yes.

He is running his eye down the columns. **Peacey** *leans over the letters.*

Peacey   This is from Mr Leader about the codicil . . . You'll answer that?

Mr Voysey   Mr Leader. Yes. Alguazils. Mr Edward's here, I suppose.

Peacey   No, sir.

Mr Voysey (*his eye twisting with some sharpness*)   What!

Peacey (*almost alarmed*)   I beg pardon, sir.

Mr Voysey   Mr Edward.

Peacey   Oh, yes, sir, been in his room some time. I thought you said Headley; he's not due back till Thursday.

Mr Voysey *discards* The Times *and sits to his desk and his letters.*

Mr Voysey   Tell Mr Edward I've come.

Peacey   Yes, sir. Anything else?

Mr Voysey   Not for the moment. Cold morning, isn't it?

Peacey   Quite surprising, sir.

Mr Voysey   We had a touch of frost down at Chislehurst.

Peacey   So early!

Mr Voysey   I want it for the celery. All right, I'll call through about the rest of the letters.

Peacey *goes, having secured a letter or two, and* **Mr Voysey** *having sorted the rest (a proportion into the wastepaper basket) takes up the forgotten roses and starts setting them into a bowl with an artistic hand. Then his son* **Edward** *comes in.* **Mr Voysey** *gives him one glance and goes on arranging the roses, but says cheerily . . .*

Mr Voysey   Good morning, my dear boy.

Edward *has little of his father in him and that little is undermost. It is a refined face, but self-consciousness takes the place in it of imagination, and in suppressing traits of brutality in his character it looks as if the young man had suppressed his sense of humour too. But whether or no, that would not be much in evidence now, for* **Edward** *is obviously going through some experience which is scaring him (there is no better word). He looks not to have slept for a night or two, and his standing there, clutching and unclutching the bundle of papers he carries, his eyes on his father, half-appealingly but half-accusingly too, his whole being altogether so unstrung and desperate, makes* **Mr Voysey**'s *uninterrupted arranging of the flowers seem very calculated indeed. At last the little tension of silence is broken.*

Edward   Father . . .

Mr Voysey   Well?

Edward   I'm glad to see you.

This is a statement of fact. He doesn't know that the commonplace phrase sounds ridiculous at such a moment.

Mr Voysey   I see you've the papers there.

Edward   Yes.

Mr Voysey   You've been through them?

Edward   As you wished me.

Mr Voysey   Well?

Edward *doesn't answer. Reference to the papers seems to overwhelm him with shame.* **Mr Voysey** *goes on with cheerful impatience.*

Mr Voysey   Now, now, my dear boy, don't take it like this. You're puzzled and worried, of course. But why didn't you come down to me on Saturday night? I expected you . . . I told you to come. Your mother was wondering why you weren't with us for dinner yesterday.

Edward   I went through everything twice. I wanted to make quite sure.

Mr Voysey   I told you to come to me.

Edward (*he is very near crying*)   Oh, Father!

Mr Voysey   Now look here, Edward, I'm going to ring and dispose of these letters. Please pull yourself together.

He pushes the little button on his table.

Edward   I didn't leave my rooms all day yesterday.

Mr Voysey   A pleasant Sunday! You must learn, whatever the business may be, to leave it behind you at the office. Life's not worth living else.

Peacey *comes in to find* **Mr Voysey** *before the fire, ostentatiously warming and rubbing his hands.*

Mr Voysey   Oh, there isn't much else, Peacey. Tell Simmons that if he satisfies you about the details of this lease it'll be all right. Make a note for me of Mr Granger's address at Mentone.

Peacey   Mr Burnett . . . Burnett and Marks . . . has just come in, Mr Edward.

Edward (*without turning*)   It's only fresh instructions. Will you take them?

Peacey   All right.

Peacey *goes, lifting his eyebrows at the queerness of* **Edward***'s manner. This* **Mr Voysey** *sees, returning to his table with a little scowl.*

Mr Voysey   Now sit down. I've given you a bad forty-eight hours, have I? Well, I've been anxious about you. Never mind, we'll thresh the thing out now. Go through the two accounts. Mrs Murberry's first . . . how do you find it stands?

Edward (*his feelings choking him*)   I hoped you were playing some joke on me.

Mr Voysey   Come now.

Edward *separates the papers precisely and starts to detail them, his voice quite toneless. Now and then his father's sharp comments ring out in contrast.*

Edward   We've got the lease of her present house, several agreements . . . and here's her will. Here's an expired power of attorney . . . over her securities and her property generally . . . it was made out for six months.

Mr Voysey   She was in South Africa.

Edward   Here's the Sheffield mortgage and the Henry Smith mortgage with banker's receipts . . . her banker's to use for the interest up to date . . . four and a half and five per cent. Then . . . Fretworthy Bonds. There's a note scribbled in your writing that they are at the bank; but you don't say what bank.

Mr Voysey   My own.

Edward (*just dwelling on the words*)   Your own, I queried that. There's eight thousand five hundred in three and a half India stock. And there are her banker's receipts for cheques on account of those dividends. I presume for those dividends.

Mr Voysey   Why not?

Edward (*gravely*)   Because then, Father, there are her banker's half-yearly receipts for other sums amounting to an average of four hundred and twenty pounds a year. But I find no record of any capital to produce this.

Mr Voysey   Go on. What do you find?

Edward   Till about three years back there seems to have been eleven thousand in Queenslands which would produce . . . d i d produce exactly the same sum. But after January of that year I find no record of them.

Mr Voysey   In fact the Queenslands are missing, vanished?

Edward (*hardly uttering the word*)   Yes.

Mr Voysey   From which you conclude?

Edward   I supposed at first that you had not handed me all the papers.

Mr Voysey   Since Mrs Murberry evidently still gets that four twenty a year, somehow; lucky woman.

Edward (*in agony*)   Oh!

Mr Voysey   Well, we'll return to the good lady later. Now let's take the other.

Edward   The Hatherley Trust.

Mr Voysey   Quite so.

Edward (*with one accusing glance*)   Trust.

Mr Voysey   Go on.

Edward   Father . . .

His grief comes uppermost again and **Mr Voysey** *meets it kindly.*

Mr Voysey   I know, my dear boy. I shall have lots to say to you. But let's get quietly through with these details first.

Edward (*bitterly now*)   Oh, this is simple enough. We're young Hatherley's trustees till he comes of age. The property was thirty-eight thousand invested in Consols. Certain sums were to be allowed for his education; we seem to be paying them.

Mr Voysey   Regularly?

Edward   Quite. But where's the capital?

Mr Voysey   No record?

Edward   Yes . . . a note by you on a half sheet: 'Refer Bletchley Land Scheme'.

Mr Voysey   Oh . . . we've been out of that six years or more! He's credited with the interest on his capital?

Edward   With the Consol interest.

Mr Voysey   Quite so.

Edward   The Bletchley scheme paid seven and a half.

Mr Voysey At one time. Have you taken the trouble to calculate what will be due from us to the lad?

Edward Yes . . . capital and interest . . . about forty-six thousand pounds.

Mr Voysey A respectable sum. In five years' time?

Edward When he comes of age.

Mr Voysey That gives us, say, four years and six months in which to think about it.

Edward *waits, hopelessly, for his father to speak again; then says . . .*

Edward Thank you for showing me these, sir. Shall I put them back in your safe now?

Mr Voysey Yes, you'd better. There's the key.

Edward *reaches for the bunch, his face hidden.*

Mr Voysey Put them down. Your hand shakes . . . why, you might have been drinking. I'll put them away later. It's no use having hysterics, Edward. Look your trouble in the face.

Edward's *only answer is to go to the fire, as far from his father as the room allows. And there he leans on the mantelpiece, his shoulders heaving.*

Mr Voysey I'm sorry, my dear boy. I wouldn't tell you if I could help it.

Edward I can't believe it. And that you should be telling me . . . such a thing.

Mr Voysey Let yourself go . . . have your cry out, as the women say. It isn't pleasant, I know. It isn't pleasant to inflict it on you.

Edward (*able to turn to his father again; won round by the kind voice*) How long has it been going on? Why didn't you tell me before? Oh, I know you thought you'd pull through. But I'm your partner . . . I'm responsible too. Oh, I don't want to shirk that . . . don't think I mean to shirk that, Father. Perhaps I ought to have discovered . . . but those affairs were always in your hands. I trusted . . . I beg your pardon. Oh, it's us . . . not you. Everyone has trusted us.

Mr Voysey (*calmly and kindly still*)   You don't seem to notice that I'm not breaking my heart like this.

Edward   What's the extent of . . . ? Are there other accounts . . . ? When did it begin? Father, what made you begin it?

Mr Voysey   I didn't begin it.

Edward   You didn't? Who then?

Mr Voysey   My father before me.

Edward *stares.*

Mr Voysey   That calms you a little.

Edward   But how terrible! Oh, my dear Father . . . I'm glad. But . . .

Mr Voysey (*shaking his head*)   My inheritance, Edward.

Edward   My dear Father!

Mr Voysey   I had hoped it wasn't to be yours.

Edward   But you mean to tell me that this sort of thing has been going on here for years? For more than thirty years!

Mr Voysey   Yes.

Edward   That's a little hard to understand . . . just at first, sir.

Mr Voysey (*sententiously*)   We do what we must in this world, Edward. I have done what I had to do.

Edward (*his emotion well cooled by now*)   Perhaps I'd better just listen while you explain.

Mr Voysey (*concentrating*)   You know that I'm heavily into Northern Electrics.

Edward   Yes.

Mr Voysey   But you don't know how heavily. When I got the tip the municipalities were organising the purchase, I saw of course the stock must be up to a hundred and forty-five – a hundred and fifty in no time. Now Leeds has quarrelled with the rural group . . . there'll be no general settlement for ten years. I bought at ninety-five. What are they today?

Edward   Seventy-two.

Mr Voysey   Seventy-one and a half. And in ten years I may be . . . ! I'm not a young man, Edward. That's mainly why you've had to be told.

Edward   With whose money are you so heavily into Northern Electrics?

Mr Voysey   The firm's money.

Edward   Clients' money?

Mr Voysey   Yes.

Edward (*coldly*)   Well . . . I'm waiting for your explanation, sir.

Mr Voysey (*with a shrug*)   Children always think the worst of their parents, I suppose. I did of mine. It's a pity.

Edward   Go on, sir, go on. Let me know the worst.

Mr Voysey   There's no immediate danger. I should think anyone could see that from the figures there. There's no real risk at all.

Edward   Is that the worst?

Mr Voysey (*his anger rising*)   Have you studied these two accounts or have you not?

Edward   Yes, sir.

Mr Voysey   Well, where's the deficiency in Mrs Murberry's income . . . has she ever gone without a shilling? What has young Hatherley lost?

Edward   He stands to lose . . .

Mr Voysey   He stands to lose nothing if I'm spared for a little, and you will only bring a little common sense to bear and try to understand the difficulties of my position.

Edward   Father, I'm not thinking ill of you . . . that is, I'm trying not to. But won't you explain how you're justified . . . ?

Mr Voysey   In putting our affairs in order?

Edward   Are you doing that?

Mr Voysey   What else?

Edward (*starting patiently to examine the matter*)   How bad were things when you came into control?

Mr Voysey   Oh, I forget.

Edward   You can't forget.

Mr Voysey   Well . . . pretty bad.

Edward   How was it my grandfather . . . ?

Mr Voysey   Muddlement . . . timidity! Had a perfect mania for petty speculation. He'd no capital . . . no real credit, and he went in terror of his life. My dear Edward, if I hadn't found out in time, he'd have confessed to the first man who came and asked for a balance sheet.

Edward   How much was he to the bad, then?

Mr Voysey   Oh . . . a tidy sum.

Edward   But it can't have taken all these years to pay off . . .

Mr Voysey   Oh, hasn't it!

Edward (*making his point*)   Then how does it happen, sir, that such a recent trust as young Hatherley's has been broken into?

Mr Voysey   Well, what could be safer? There is no one to interfere, and we haven't to settle up for five years.

Edward (*utterly beaten*)   Father, are you mad?

Mr Voysey   Mad? I wish everybody were as sane. As a trustee the law permits me to earn for a fluid three and a half per cent . . . and that I do . . . punctually and safely. Now as to Mrs Murberry . . . those Fretworthy Bonds at my bank . . . I've borrowed five thousand on them. But I can release them tomorrow if need be.

Edward   Where's the five thousand?

Mr Voysey   I needed it . . . temporarily . . . to complete a purchase . . . there was that and four thousand more out of the Skipworth fund.

Edward   But, my dear Father –

Mr Voysey   Well?

Edward (*summing it all up very simply*)   It's not right.

Mr Voysey *considers his son for a moment with a pitying shake of the head.*

Mr Voysey   That is a word, Edward, which one should learn to use very carefully. You mean that from time to time I have had to go beyond the letter of the law. But consider the position I found myself in. Was I to see my father ruined and disgraced without lifting a finger to help him? I paid back to the man who was most involved in my father's mistakes every penny of his capital . . . and he never even knew the danger he'd been in . . . never had one uneasy moment. It was I that lay awake. I have now somewhere a letter from that man written as he lay dying . . . I'll tell you who it was, old Thomson the physiologist . . . saying that only his perfect confidence in our conduct of his affairs had enabled him to do his life's work in peace. Well, Edward, I went beyond the letter of the law to do that service . . . to my father . . . to old Thomson . . . to Science . . . to Humanity. Was I right or wrong?

Edward   In the result, sir, right.

Mr Voysey   Judge me by the result. I took the risk of failure I should have suffered. I could have kept clear of the danger if I'd liked.

Edward   But that's all past. The thing that concerns me is what you are doing now.

Mr Voysey (*gently reproachful*)   My boy, can't you trust me a little? It's all very well for you to come in at the end of the day and criticise. But I who have done the day's work know how that work had to be done. And here's our firm, prosperous, respected and without a stain on its honour. That's the main point, isn't it?

Edward (*quite irresponsive to this pathetic appeal*)   Very well, sir. Let's dismiss from our minds any prejudice about behaving as honest firms of solicitors do behave . . .

Mr Voysey   We need to do nothing of the sort. If a man gives me definite instructions about his property I follow them. And more often than not he suffers.

Edward   But if Mrs Murberry knew . . .

Mr Voysey   Well, if you can make her understand her affairs . . . financial or other . . . it's more than I ever could. Go and knock it into her head, then, if you can, that four hundred and twenty pounds of her income hasn't, for the last eight years, come from the place she thinks it's come from, and see how happy you'll make her.

Edward   But is that four hundred and twenty a year as safe as it was before you . . . ?

Mr Voysey   Why not?

Edward   What's the security?

Mr Voysey (*putting his coping stone on the argument*)   My financial ability.

Edward (*really not knowing whether to laugh or cry*)   Why, one'd think you were satisfied with this state of things.

Mr Voysey   Edward, you really are most unsympathetic and unreasonable. I give all I have to the firm's work . . . my brain . . . my energies . . . my whole life. I can't, so to speak, cash in my abilities at par . . . I wish I could. If I could establish every one of these people with a separate and consistent bank balance tomorrow . . . naturally I should do it.

Edward (*thankfully able to meet anger with anger*)   Do you mean to tell me that you couldn't somehow have put things straight before now?

Mr Voysey   So easy to talk, isn't it?

Edward   If thirty years of this sort of thing hasn't brought you hopelessly to grief . . . why, there must have been opportunities . . .

Mr Voysey   Must there! Well, I hope that when I'm under the ground, you may find them.

Edward   I?

Mr Voysey   And put everything right with a stroke of your pen, if it's so easy!

Edward   I!

Mr Voysey   You're my partner and my son. You inherit the problem.

Edward (*realising at last that he has been led to the edge of this abyss*) Oh no, Father.

Mr Voysey   Why else have I had to tell you all this?

Edward (*very simply*)   Father, I can't. I can't possibly. I don't think you've any right to ask me.

Mr Voysey   Why not, pray?

Edward   It's perpetuating the dishonesty.

Mr Voysey *hardens at the unpleasant word.*

Mr Voysey   You don't believe that I've told you the truth.

Edward   I want to believe it.

Mr Voysey   It's no proof . . . my earning these twenty or thirty people their incomes for the last . . . how many years?

Edward   Whether what you've done has been wrong or right . . . I can't meddle in it.

For the moment **Mr Voysey** *looks a little dangerous.*

Mr Voysey   Very well. Forget all I've said. Go back to your room. Get back to your drudgery. A life's work – my life's work – ruined! What does that matter?

Edward   Whatever did you expect of me?

Mr Voysey (*making a feint at his papers*)   Oh, nothing. (*Then he slams them down with great effect.*) Here's a great edifice built up by years of labour and devotion and self-sacrifice . . . a great arch you may call it . . . a bridge to carry our firm to safety with honour. My work! And it still lacks the keystone. Just that! And it may be I am to die with my work incomplete. Then is there nothing that a son might do? Do you think I shouldn't be proud of you, Edward . . . that I shouldn't bless you from . . . wherever I may be, when you had completed my life's work . . . with perhaps just one kindly thought of your father?

In spite of this oratory, the situation is gradually impressing **Edward**.

Edward   What will happen if I leave the firm now?

Mr Voysey   I shall see that you are not held responsible.

Edward   I wasn't thinking of myself, sir.

Mr Voysey   Well, I shan't mind the exposure. It won't make me blush in my coffin. And you're not so quixotic, I hope, as to be thinking of the feelings of your brothers and sisters. Considering how simple it would have been for me to go to my grave and let you discover the whole thing afterwards, the fact that I didn't, that I take thought for the future of you all . . . well, I did hope it might convince you that I . . . ! But there . . . consult your own safety.

Edward *has begun to pace the room; indecision growing upon him.*

Edward   It's a queer dilemma to be facing.

Mr Voysey   My dear boy . . . don't think I can't appreciate the shock it has been to you. After all, I had to go through it, you know. And worse!

Edward   Why worse?

Mr Voysey   Well . . . I was a bit younger. And my poor dear dad was on the edge of the precipice . . . all but over it. I'm not landing you in any such mess, Edward. On the contrary! On the contrary!

Edward   Yes, I came this morning thinking that next week would see us in the dock together.

Mr Voysey   And I suppose if I'd broken down and begged your pardon for my folly, you'd have done anything for me, gone to prison smiling, eh?

Edward   I suppose so.

Mr Voysey   Oh, it's easy enough to forgive. I'm sorry I can't assume sackcloth and ashes to oblige you. (*Now he begins to rally his son; easy in his strength.*) My dear Edward, you've lived a quiet humdrum life up to now, with your poetry and your sociology and your agnosticism and your ethics of this and your ethics of that! . . . and you've never before been brought face to face with any really vital question. Now don't make a fool of yourself just through inexperience. I'm not angry at what you've said to me. I'm willing to forget it. And it's for your own sake and not for mine, Edward, that I do beg you to . . . to . . . be a man and take a man's view of the position you find yourself in. It's not a pleasant position, I know . . . but we must take this world as we find it, my dear boy.

Edward   You should have told me before you took me into partnership.

Oddly enough it is this last flicker of rebellion which breaks down **Mr Voysey**'s *caution. Now he lets fly with a vengeance.*

Mr Voysey   Should I be telling you at all if I could help it? Don't I know you're about as fit for the job as a babe unborn? I've been hoping and praying for these three years past that you'd show signs of shaping into something. But I'm in a corner . . . and am I to see things come to smash simply because of your scruples? If you're a son of mine you'll do as I tell you. Hadn't I the same choice to make? D'you suppose I didn't have scruples? If you run away from this, Edward, you're a coward. My father was a coward and he suffered for it to the end of his days. I was more of a sick-nurse to him here than a partner. Good Lord! . . . of course it's pleasant and comfortable to keep within the law . . . then the law will look after you. Otherwise you have to look pretty sharp after yourself. You have to cultivate your own sense of right and wrong . . . deal your own justice. But that makes a bigger man of you, let me tell you. How easily . . . how easily could I have walked out of my father's office and left him to his fate! But I didn't. I thought it my better duty to stay and . . . yes, I say it with all reverence . . . to take up my cross. Well, I've carried that cross pretty successfully. And what's more, it's made a happy . . . a self-respecting man of me. I don't want what I've been saying to influence you, Edward. You are a free agent. You must consult your conscience and decide upon your own course of action. Now don't let's discuss the matter any more for the moment.

Edward *looks at his father with clear eyes.*

Edward   Don't forget to put these papers away.

Mr Voysey   Are you coming down to Chislehurst soon? We've got Hugh and his wife, and Booth and Emily, and Christopher for two or three days, till he goes back to school.

Edward   How is Chris?

Mr Voysey   All right again now . . . grows more like his father. Booth's very proud of him. So am I.

Edward   I think I can't face them all just at present.

Mr Voysey   Nonsense.

Edward (*a little wave of emotion going through him*)   I feel as if this thing were written on my face. How I shall get through business I don't know!

Mr Voysey   You're weaker than I thought, Edward.

Edward (*a little ironically*)   I've always wondered why I was such a disappointment to you, Father. Though you've been very kind about it.

Mr Voysey   No, no. I say things I don't mean sometimes.

Edward   You should have brought one of the others into the firm. Trenchard or Booth.

Mr Voysey (*hardening*)   Trenchard! (*He dismisses that.*) Heavens, you're a better man than Booth. Edward, you mustn't imagine that the whole world is standing on its head merely because you've had an unpleasant piece of news. Come down to Chislehurst tonight . . . well, say tomorrow night. It'll be good for you . . . stop your brooding. That's your worst vice, Edward. You'll find the household as if nothing had happened. Then you'll remember that nothing really has happened. And presently you'll see that nothing need happen, if you keep your head. I remember times . . . when things have seemed at their worst . . . what a relief it's been to me . . . my romp with you all in the nursery just before your bedtime. And, my dear boy, if I knew that you were going to inform the next client you met of what I've just told you . . .

Edward (*with a shudder*)   Father!

Mr Voysey   . . . and that I should find myself in prison tomorrow, I wouldn't wish a single thing I've ever done undone. I have never wilfully harmed man or woman. My life's been a happy one. Your dear mother has been spared to me. You're most of you good children and a credit to what I've done for you.

Edward (*the deadly humour of this too much for him*)   Father!

Mr Voysey   Run along now, run along. I must finish my letters and get into the City.

He might be scolding a schoolboy for some trifling fault. **Edward** *turns to have a look at the keen, unembarrassed face.* **Mr Voysey** *smiles at him and proceeds to select from the bowl a rose for his buttonhole.*

Edward   I'll think it over, sir.

Mr Voysey   That's right! And don't brood.

So **Edward** *leaves him; and having fixed the rose in his buttonhole to his satisfaction he rings his table telephone and calls through to the listening clerk.*

Mr Voysey   Send Atkinson to me, please.

Then he gets up, keys in hand, to lock away Mrs Murberry's and the Hatherley Trust papers.

Act Two

*The Voysey dining room at Chislehurst, when children and grandchildren
are visiting, is dining table and very little else. And at the moment in the
evening when five or six men are sprawling back in their chairs, and the
air is clouded with smoke, it is a very typical specimen of the middle-class
English domestic temple. It has the usual red-papered walls, the usual
varnished woodwork which is known as grained oak; there is the usual
hot, mahogany furniture; and, commanding point of the whole room, there
is the usual black-marble sarcophagus of a fireplace. Above this hangs one
of the two or three oil paintings, which are all that break the red pattern
of the walls: the portrait, painted in 1880, of an undistinguished-looking
gentleman aged sixty; he is shown sitting in a more graceful attitude than
it could ever have been comfortable for him to assume.* **Mr Voysey**'s
*father it is, and the brass plate at the bottom of the frame tells us that the
portrait was a presentation one. On the mantelpiece stands, of course, a
clock; at either end a china vase filled with paper spills. And in front of
the fire – since that is the post of vantage – stands at this moment*
Major Booth Voysey. *He is the second son, of the age that it is
necessary for a Major to be, and of the appearance of many ordinary
Majors in ordinary regiments. He went into the Army because he thought
it would come up to a schoolboy's idea of it; and, being there, he does his
little all to keep it to this. He stands astride, hands in pockets, coat-tails
through his arms, half-smoked cigar in mouth, moustache bristling. On
either side of him sits at the table an old gentleman; the one is* **Mr Evan
Colpus**, *the vicar of their parish, the other* **Mr George Booth**, *a
friend of long standing, and the* **Major**'s *godfather.* **Mr Colpus** *is a
harmless enough anachronism, except for the comparative waste of £400
a year in which his stipend involves the community. Leaving most of his
parochial work to an energetic curate, he devotes his serious attention to the
composition of two sermons a week.* **Mr Booth**, *on the contrary, is as
gay an old gentleman as can be found in Chislehurst. An only son, his
father left him at the age of twenty-five a fortune of a hundred thousand
pounds. At the same time he had the good sense to dispose of his father's
business, into which he had been most unwillingly introduced five years
earlier, for a like sum before he was able to depreciate its value. It was*
Mr Voysey's *invaluable assistance in this transaction which first bound*

the two together in great friendship. Since that time **Mr Booth** *has been bent on nothing but enjoying himself. He has even remained a bachelor with that object. Money has given him all he wants, therefore he loves and reverences money; while his imagination may be estimated by the fact that he has now reached the age of sixty-five, still possessing more of it than he knows what to do with. At the head of the table, meditatively cracking walnuts, sits* **Mr Voysey**. *He has his back to the conservatory door. On* **Mr Voysey**'s *left is* **Denis Tregoning**, *a nice enough young man. And at the other end of the table sits* **Edward**, *not smoking, not talking, hardly listening, very depressed. Behind him is the ordinary door of the room, which leads out into the dismal, draughty hall. The* **Major**'s *voice is like the sound of a cannon through the tobacco smoke.*

Major Booth Voysey   Certainly . . . I am hot and strong for conscription . . . and the question will be to the fore again very shortly.

Mr George Booth   My dear boy . . . the country won't hear of it . . .

Major Booth Voysey   I differ from you. If we . . . the Army . . . if the men who have studied the subject . . . the brains of the Army . . . say as one man to the country: Conscription is once more necessary for your safety . . . what answer has the country? What? There you are! None.

Tregoning   You try . . . and you'll see.

Major Booth Voysey   If the international situation grows more threatening I shall seriously consider going on half-pay for a bit and entering the House. And . . . I'm not a conceited man . . . but I believe that if I speak out upon a subject I understand, and only upon that subject, the House . . and the country . . . will listen.

Mr George Booth   The gentlemen of England have always risen to an emergency. Why . . . old as I am . . . I would shoulder a musket myself if need be. But . . .

Major Booth Voysey   Just one moment. Our national safety is not the only question. There's the stamina of the race . . . deplorably deteriorated! You should just see the fellars that try

to enlist nowadays. Horrid little runts . . . with their stinkin'
little fags . . . hangin' out of the corners of their slobberin'
little mouths. What England wants is chest. Chest and
discipline. And conscription . . .

Mr Voysey (*with the crack of a nut*)   Your godson talks a deal,
don't he? You know, when our Major gets into a club, he gets
on the committee . . . gets on any committee to inquire into
anything . . . and then goes on at 'em just like this. Don't you,
Booth?

The **Major** *knuckles under easily enough to his father's sarcasm.*

Major Booth Voysey   Well, sir, people tell me I'm a useful
man on committees.

Mr Voysey   I don't doubt it . . . your voice must drown all
discussion.

Major Booth Voysey   You can't say I don't listen to you, sir.

Mr Voysey   I don't . . . and I'm not blaming you. But I must
say I often think what a devil of a time the family will have
with you when I'm gone. Fortunately for your poor mother,
she's deaf.

Major Booth Voysey   Well, sir . . . it might be my duty as
eldest son . . . Trenchard not counting . . .

Mr Voysey (*with the crack of another nut*)   Trenchard not
counting. Oh, certainly . . . bully them. Never mind whether
you're right or wrong . . . bully them, I don't manage things
that way myself, but I think it's your best chance.

Major Booth Voysey (*with some discomfort*)   Ha! If I were a
conceited man, sir, I could trust you to take it out of me.

Mr Voysey (*as he taps* **Mr George Booth** *with the nut-crackers*)
Help yourself, George, and drink to your godson's health. Long
may he keep his chest notes! Never heard him on parade, have
you?

Tregoning   There's one thing you learn in the Army . . . and
that's how to display yourself. Booth makes a perfect firescreen.
But I believe after mess that position is positively rushed.

Major Booth Voysey (*cheered to find an opponent he can tackle*)
If you want a bit of fire, say so, you sucking Lord Chancellor.
Because I mean to allow you to be my brother-in-law, you
think you can be impertinent.

So **Tregoning** *moves to the fire and that changes the conversation.*

Mr Voysey   Vicar, the port's with you. Help yourself and
send it on.

Mr Colpus   Thank you . . . I have had my quantum.

Mr Voysey   Nonsense!

Mr Colpus   Well . . . a teeny weeny dram!

Mr Voysey   By the way . . . did you see Lady Mary
yesterday? Is she going to help us clear off the debt on the
chapel?

Mr Colpus   Well, no . . . I'm afraid she isn't.

Mr Voysey   Why not?

Mr Colpus   Well . . . the fact is, she's quite angry.

Mr Voysey   What about?

Mr Colpus   I regret to tell you . . . it's about Hugh's fresco.

Major Booth Voysey   Ah . . . I knew there'd be trouble!

Mr Colpus   Someone has let it out to her that the Apostles
are all portraits of people . . . and she strongly disapproves.

Major Booth Voysey   So do I.

Mr Colpus   Indeed, I fear she's writing to you to say that as
Hugh is your son she thinks you should have kept him under
better control. I said I'd done all I could. And I did argue with
him. First of all, you know, he wanted to make them local
people . . . the butcher and the plumber and old Sandford. He
said the fifteenth-century Florentines always did it. I said: 'My
dear Hugh, we are not fifteenth-century Florentines.'

Major Booth Voysey   Hugh's no good at a likeness. I don't
believe anyone would have known.

Mr Colpus   But all he said was: 'Ha! Ha!' Then I didn't see the thing for a week, and . . . oh, far worse! . . . he'd made them all quite well-known public characters! And as it was in tempera, he couldn't alter it without taking the wall down.

Mr Voysey   What's the debt now?

Mr Colpus   Three hundred pounds nearly.

Mr Voysey   I shall have to stump up, I suppose.

Major Booth Voysey   Anonymously. What?

Mr Voysey   George Booth . . . will you go halves?

Mr George Booth   Certainly not. I can't see what we wanted the chapel at all for. Eight hundred pounds and more . . . !

Mr Colpus   People do drop in and pray. Oh . . . I've seen them.

Mr George Booth   Well, Vicar . . . it's your business, of course . . . but I call it a mistake to encourage all this extra religion. Work on weekdays . . . church on Sundays. That was the rule when I was young.

Mr Voysey   You can't stop people praying.

Mr George Booth   But why make a show of it? What's the result? Hugh's a case in point. When he was a boy . . . mad about religion! Used to fast on Fridays! I remember your punishing him for it. Now look at him. What his beliefs are now . . . well, I'd rather not know. And with Edward here . . .

Edward   With me?

Mr George Booth   Up at Cambridge . . . wanted to turn Papist, didn't you? And now . . . I suppose you call yourself a free-thinker.

Edward   I don't call myself anything.

Mr George Booth   Keep to the middle of the road . . . that's what I'd tell any young man.

Tregoning   Safety first.

Mr George Booth   Certainly. For what should be a man's aim in life? I have always known mine, and . . . though far be it from me to boast . . . I look back to nothing I need regret . . . nothing the whole world might not know. I don't speak of quite personal affairs. Like most other men, I have been young. But all that sort of thing is nobody's business but one's own. I inherited a modest fortune. I have not needed to take the bread out of other men's mouths by working. My money has been wisely administered . . . well, ask your father about that . . . and has . . . not diminished. I have paid my taxes without grumbling. I have never wronged any man. I have never lied about anything that mattered. I have left theories to take care of themselves and tried to live the life of an English gentleman. And I consider there is no higher . . . at any rate no more practical ideal.

Major Booth Voysey (*not to be outdone by this display of virtue*) Well, I'm not a conceited man, but –

Tregoning   I hope you're sure of that, Booth.

Major Booth Voysey   Shut up. I was going to say, when my young cub of a brother-in-law-to-be interrupted me, that training, for which we all have to be thankful to you, sir, has much to do with it. (*Suddenly he pulls his trousers against his legs.*) I say, I'm scorching. Try one of those new cigars, Denis?

Tregoning   No, thank you.

Major Booth Voysey   I will.

He glances round. **Tregoning** *sees a box on the table and reaches it.* **Mr Colpus** *gets up.*

Mr Colpus   Must be taking my departure.

Mr Voysey   Already!

Major Booth Voysey (*frowning upon the cigar-box*) No, not those. The Ramon Allones. Why on earth doesn't Honor see they're here?

Mr Voysey   Spare time for a chat with my wife before you go. She had ideas about a children's tea-fight.

Mr Colpus   Certainly I will.

Major Booth Voysey (*scowling helplessly around*)   My
goodness! . . . one can never find anything in this house.

Mr Voysey   My regards to Mrs Colpus. Hope her lumbago
will be better.

Mr Colpus   These trials are sent us.

He is sliding through the half-opened door when **Ethel** *meets him,
flinging it wide. She is the younger daughter, the baby of the family, but
twenty-three now.*

Mr Voysey   I say! It's cold again tonight! An ass of an
architect who built this place . . . such a draught between these
two doors.

He gets up to draw the curtain, When he turns **Mr Colpus** *has
disappeared, while* **Ethel** *has been followed into the room by* **Alice
Maitland**, *who shuts the door after her.* **Miss Alice Maitland** *is
a young lady of any age to thirty. Nor need her appearance alter for the
next fifteen years, since her nature is healthy and well-balanced. It mayn't
be a pretty face, but it has alertness and humour; and the resolute eyes and
eyebrows are a more innocent edition of* **Mr Voysey**'s, *who is her uncle.*
Ethel *goes straight to her father (though her glance is on* **Denis** *and his
on her) and chirps, birdlike, in her spoiled-child way . . .*

Ethel   We think you've stayed in here quite long enough.

Mr Voysey   That's to say, Ethel thinks Denis has been kept
out of her pocket much too long.

Ethel   Ethel wants billiards . . . Father . . . what a dessert
you've eaten. Greedy pig!

Alice *is standing behind* **Edward**, *considering his hair-parting
apparently.*

Alice   Crack me a filbert, please, Edward . . . I had none.

Edward (*jumping up, rather formally well-mannered*)   I beg your
pardon, Alice. Won't you sit down?

Alice   No.

Mr Voysey (*taking* **Ethel** *on his knee*)   Come here, puss. Have you made up your mind yet what you want for a wedding present?

Ethel (*rectifying a stray hair on his forehead*)   After mature consideration, I decide on a cheque.

Mr Voysey   Do you!

Ethel   Yes. I think that a cheque will give most scope to your generosity. If you desire to add any trimmings in the shape of a piano or a Persian carpet you may . . . and Denis and I will be grateful. But I think I'd let yourself go over a cheque.

Mr Voysey   You're a minx.

Major Booth Voysey (*giving up the cigar search*)   Here, who's going to play?

Mr George Booth (*pathetically, as he gets up*)   Well, if my wrist will hold out.

Major Booth Voysey (*to* **Tregoning**)   No, don't you bother to look for them. (*He strides from the room, his voice echoing through the hall.*) Honor, where are those Ramon Allones?

Alice (*calling after*)   She's in the drawing room with Auntie and Mr Colpus.

Mr Voysey   Now I suggest that you and Denis go and take off the billiard-table cover. You'll find folding it up a very excellent amusement.

He illustrates his meaning with his table napkin and by putting together the tips of his forefingers, roguishly.

Mr George Booth   Ah ha! I remember that being done in some play . . .

Ethel   Dear Father . . . you must try not to be roguish. You won't get a blush or a giggle out of either of us. Denis . . . come here and kiss me . . . before everybody.

Tregoning   I shall do nothing of the sort.

Ethel   If you don't I swear I won't marry you. Come along. I detest self-conscious people. Come on.

Denis *gives her a shamefaced peck on one cheek.*

Ethel   That's a nice sort of kiss, too! If it wasn't for having to send back the presents I wouldn't marry you.

She goes off.

Tregoning   Women have no shame.

The **Major** *comes stalking back, followed in a fearful flurry by his elder sister,* **Honor**. **Denis** *follows* **Ethel**. *Poor* **Honor** *(her female friends are apt to refer to her as 'Poor Honor') is a phenomenon common to most large families. From her earliest years she has been bottle-washer to her brothers. They were expensively educated, but she was grudged schooling. Her fate is a curious survival of the intolerance of parents towards daughters until the vanity of their hunger for sons has been gratified. In a less humane society she would have been exposed at birth. Yet* **Honor** *is not unhappy in her survival, even if at this moment her life is a burden.*

Major Booth Voysey   Honor, they are not in the dining room.

Honor   But they m u s t be! – where else c a n they be?

She has a habit of accentuating one word in each sentence and often the wrong one.

Major Booth Voysey   That's what you ought to know.

Mr Voysey *(as he moves towards the door)*   Well . . . will you have a game?

Mr George Booth   I'll play you fifty up, not more, I'm getting old.

Mr Voysey *(stopping at a dessert dish)*   Yes, these are good apples of Bearman's. Six of my trees spoilt this year.

Honor   Here you are, Booth.

She triumphantly discovers the discarded box, at which the **Major** *becomes pathetic with indignation.*

Major Booth Voysey   Oh, Honor, don't be such a fool.
I want the Ramon Allones

Honor   I don't know the difference.

Major Booth Voysey   No, you don't, but you might learn.

Mr Voysey (*in a voice like the crack of a very fine whip*)   Booth!

Major Booth Voysey (*subduedly*)   What is it, sir?

Mr Voysey   Look for your cigars yourself. Honor, go back to
your reading or your sewing or whatever you were fiddling at,
and fiddle in peace.

Mr Voysey *departs, leaving the room rather hushed.* **Mr Booth** *has
not waited for this parental display.* Then **Alice** *insinuates a remark very
softly.*

Alice   Have you looked in the library?

Major Booth Voysey (*relapsing to an injured mutter*)   Where's
Emily?

Honor   Upstairs with little Henry; he woke up and cried.

Major Booth Voysey   Letting her wear herself to rags over
the child . . .

Honor   Well, she won't let m e go.

Major Booth Voysey   Why don't you stop looking for those
cigars?

Honor   If you don't mind, I want a lace doily now I am
here.

Major Booth Voysey   I daresay they're in the library. What
a house!

He departs.

Honor   Booth is so trying.

Alice   Honor, why do you put up with it?

Honor   Someone has to.

Alice (*discreetly nibbling a nut, which* **Edward** *has cracked for her*)
I'm afraid I think Master Major Booth ought to have been
taken in hand early . . . with a cane.

Honor (*as she vaguely burrows into corners*)   Papa did. But it's
never prevented him booming at us . . . oh, ever since he was a
baby. Now he's flustered me so I simply can't remember which
set of them it was.

Alice   The Pettifers wished to be remembered to you, Edward.

Honor   I'd better take one of each. (*But she goes on looking.*) I
sometimes think, Alice, that we're a very difficult family . . .
except perhaps Edward.

Edward   Why except me?

Honor   And you were always difficult . . . to yourself. (*Then
she starts to go, threading her way through the disarranged chairs.*) Mr
Colpus will shout so at Mother, and she doesn't like people
to think she's so very deaf . . . I thought Mary Pettifer looking
old . . . (*She talks herself out of the room.*)

Alice (*after her*)   She's getting old. I was glad not to spend
August abroad for once. We drove into Cheltenham to a
dance. I golfed a lot.

Edward   How long were you with them?

Alice   A fortnight. It doesn't seem three months since I was
here.

Edward   I'm down so seldom.

Alice   I might be one of the family . . . almost.

Edward   You know they're always pleased.

Alice   Well, being a homeless person! But what a cartload to
descend . . . yesterday and today. The Major and Emily . . .
Emily's not at all well. Hugh and Mrs Hugh. And me. Are you
staying?

Edward   No. I must get a word with my father.

Alice   Edward . . . you look more like half-baked pie-crust than usual. I wish you didn't sit over your desk quite so much.

Edward (*a little enviously*)   You're very well.

Alice   I'm always well and nearly always happy.

The **Major** *returns. He has the right sort of cigar in his mouth and is considerably mollified.*

Alice   You found them?

Major Booth Voysey   Of course they were there. Thank you very much, Alice. Now I want a knife.

Alice   I must give you a cigar-cutter for Christmas, Booth.

Major Booth Voysey   Beastly things, I hate 'em, (*He eyes the dessert disparagingly.*) Nothing but silver ones.

Edward *hands him a carefully opened pocket-knife.*

Major Booth Voysey   Thank you, Edward. And I must take one of the candles. Something's gone wrong with the library ventilator and you never can see a thing in that room.

Alice   Is Mrs Hugh there?

Major Booth Voysey   Writing letters. Things are neglected here, Edward, unless one is constantly on the lookout. The Pater only cares for his garden. I must speak seriously to Honor.

He has returned the knife, still open, and having now lit his cigar at the candle he carries this off.

Edward (*giving her a nut, about the fifteenth*)   Here. 'Scuse fingers.

Alice   Thank you. (*Looking at him, with her head on one side and her face more humorous than ever.*) Edward, why have you given up proposing to me?

He starts, flushes; then won't be outdone in humour.

Edward   One can't go on proposing for ever.

Alice   Have you seen anyone you like better?

Edward   No.

Alice   Well . . . I miss it.

Edward   What satisfaction did you find in refusing me?

Alice (*as she weighs the matter*)   I find satisfaction in feeling that I'm wanted.

Edward   Without any intention of giving . . . of throwing yourself away.

Alice (*teasing his sudden earnestness*)   Ah, now we come from mere vanity to serious questions.

Edward   Mine was a very serious question.

Alice   But, Edward, all questions are serious to you. You're a perfect little pocket guide to life . . . every question answered; what to eat, drink and avoid, what to believe and what to say. Some things are worth bothering over and some aren't.

Edward   One lays down principles.

Alice   I prefer my plan. I always do what I know I want to do. Crack me another nut.

Edward   Haven't you had enough?

Alice   I know I want one more.

He cracks another with a sigh which sounds ridiculous in that connection.

I know it just as I knew I didn't want to marry you . . . each time. I didn't say no on principle . . . or because I thought it wouldn't be wise. That's why I want you to keep on asking me. Because at any moment I might say yes. And then I suppose I should find that it was simply a habit you'd got into . . . and that you didn't want me after all. Still, take another chance. Take it now!

Edward   No . . . I think not . . . now.

Alice   Edward! There's nothing wrong, is there?

Edward   Nothing at all.

They are interrupted by the sudden appearance of **Mrs Hugh Voysey**, *a brisk, bright little woman, in an evening gown which she has bullied a cheap dressmaker into making look exceedingly smart.* **Beatrice** *is hard and clever. But if she keeps her feelings buried pretty deep it is because they are precious to her; and if she is impatient with fools it is because her own brains have had to win her everything in the world, so perhaps she does overvalue them a little. She speaks always with great decision and little effort.*

Beatrice   I believe I could write business letters upon an island in the middle of Fleet Street. But while Booth is poking at a ventilator with a billiard cue . . . no, I can't. The Vicar's in the drawing room . . . and my bedroom's like an ice house.

She goes to the fireplace, waving her half-finished letter. The **Major** *appears at the door, billiard cue in hand, and says solemnly . . .*

Major Booth Voysey   Edward, I wish you'd come and have a look at this ventilator, like a good fellow.

Then he turns and goes again, obviously with the weight of an important matter on his shoulders. With the ghost of a smile **Edward** *gets up and follows him.*

Alice   No one has a right to be as good and kind as Edward is. It encourages the rotters.

With which comment she joins **Beatrice** *at the fireplace.*

Beatrice   A satisfactory day's shopping?

Alice   Mm. The baby bride and I bought clothes all the morning. Then we had lunch with Denis and bought furniture.

Beatrice   Nice furniture?

Alice   Very good and very new. They neither of them know what they want. (*Then suddenly throwing up her chin and exclaiming*) Beatrice . . . why d o women get married? Oh, of course . . . if you're caught young! With Ethel and Denis now . . . they're two little birds building their nest and it's all ideal. They'll soon forget they've ever been apart.

Now **Honor** *flutters into the room, patient but wild-eyed.*

Honor   Mother wants last week's *Notes and Queries.* Have you seen it?

Beatrice (*exasperated at the interruption*)   No.

Honor   It ought not to be here. (*So she proceeds to look for it.*) Hugh had it.

Beatrice   Lit his pipe with it.

Honor   Oh, d'you t h i n k so?

So she gives up the search and flutters out again.

Alice   This is a most unrestful house.

Beatrice   I once thought of putting the Voyseys into a book of mine. Then I concluded they'd be as dull there as they are anywhere else.

Alice   They're not duller than most of the rest of us.

Beatrice   But how very dull that is!

Alice   They're a little noisier and perhaps not quite so well-mannered. But I love them . . . in a sort of way.

Beatrice   I don't. I should have thought love was just what they couldn't inspire.

Alice   Hugh's not like the others.

Beatrice   He has most of their bad points. But I don't love Hugh.

Alice (*her eyebrows up, though she smiles*)   Beatrice, you shouldn't say so.

Beatrice   Sounds affected, doesn't it?

Alice (*her face growing a little thoughtful*)   Beatrice . . . were you in love with Hugh when you married him? Don't answer if you don't want to.

Beatrice   I married him for his money.

Alice   He hadn't much.

Beatrice   I had none . . . and I wanted to chuck journalism and write books. Yes, I loved him enough to marry him. But with some of us . . . that's not much.

Alice   But you thought you'd be happy?

Beatrice (*considering carefully*)   No, I didn't. I hoped he'd be happy. Dear Alice, how ever should you understand these things? You've eight hundred a year.

Alice   What has that to do with it?

Beatrice (*putting her case very precisely*)   Fine feelings, my dear, are as much a luxury as clean gloves. From seventeen to twenty-eight I had to earn my own living . . . and I'm no genius. So there wasn't a single thing I ever did genuinely for its own sake. No . . . always with an eye to bread-and-butter . . . pandering to the people who were to give that. I warned Hugh . . . he took the risk.

Alice   What risk?

Beatrice   That one day I'd find I could get on better without him.

Alice   And if he can't without you?

Beatrice   One should never let one's happiness depend on other people. It's degrading . . .

The conservatory door opens and through it come **Mr Voysey** *and* **Mr Booth** *in the midst of a discussion.*

Mr Voysey   My dear man, stick to the shares and risk it.

Mr George Booth   No, of course if you seriously advise me . . .

Mr Voysey   I never advise greedy children; I let 'em overeat 'emselves and take the consequences.

Alice (*shaking a finger*)   Uncle Trench, you've been in the garden without a hat after playing billiards in that hot room.

Mr George Booth   We had to give up . . . my wrist was bad. They've started pool.

Beatrice   Is Booth going to play?

Mr Voysey   We left him instructing Ethel how to hold a cue.

Beatrice   I can finish my letter.

Off she goes. **Alice** *is idly following with a little paper her hand has fallen on behind the clock.*

Mr Voysey   Don't run away, my dear.

Alice   I'm taking this to Auntie . . . *Notes and Queries* . . . she wants it.

Mr Voysey   This room's cold. Why don't they keep the fire up? (*He proceeds to put coals on it.*)

Mr George Booth   It was too hot in the billiard room. You know, Voysey . . . about those Alguazils?

Mr Voysey (*through the rattling of the coals*)   What?

Mr George Booth (*trying to pierce the din*)   Those Alguazils.

Mr Voysey *with surprising inconsequence points a finger at the silk handkerchief across* **Mr Booth**'s *shirt front.*

Mr Voysey   What have you got your handkerchief there for?

Mr George Booth   Measure of precau − (*At that moment he sneezes.*) Damn it . . . if you've given me a chill dragging me through your infernal garden.

Mr Voysey (*slapping him on the back*)   You're an old crock.

Mr George Booth   Well, I'll be glad of a winter in Egypt. (*He returns to his subject.*) And if you think seriously that I ought to sell out of the Alguazils before I go . . . ? Well . . . you'll have them. You can sell out if things look bad.

At this moment **Phoebe**, *the middle-aged parlourmaid, comes in, tray in hand. Like an expert fisherman,* **Mr Voysey** *lets loose the thread of the conversation.*

Mr Voysey   D'you want to clear?

Phoebe   It doesn't matter, sir.

Mr Voysey   No, go on . . . go on.

So **Mary**, *the young housemaid, comes in as well, and the two start to clear the table. All of which fidgets poor* **Mr Booth** *considerably. He sits shrivelled up in the armchair by the fire; and now* **Mr Voysey** *attends to him.*

Mr Voysey   George . . . I've told you again and again that you ought not to run after high interest as you do.

Mr George Booth   Yes . . . but one ought to see that one's money's put to good use.

Mr Voysey   You're an old gambler.

Mr George Booth (*propitiatingly*)   Ah, but then I've you to advise me. I do what you tell me in the end . . . you can't deny that.

Mr Voysey   The man who don't know must trust in the man who do.

Mr George Booth (*modestly insisting*)   There's ten thousand in Alguazils. What else could we put it into?

Mr Voysey   I can get you something at four and a half.

Mr George Booth   Oh, Lord!

Mr Voysey (*with a sudden serious friendliness*)   I sometimes wish, George, that you'd look after your own affairs a little more than you do. You leave far too much in my hands. If I were a crook I could play Old Harry with them . . . and I doubt if you'd ever find out.

Mr George Booth   But, of course, I shouldn't trust anybody. It's a question of knowing one's man . . . as I know you. Ah, my friend, what'll happen to your firm when you depart this life! . . . not before my time, I hope.

Mr Voysey (*with a little frown*)   What d'ye mean?

Mr George Booth   Edward's no use.

Mr Voysey   I beg your pardon . . . very sound in business.

Mr George Booth   May be . . . but I tell you he's no use. No personality.

Mr Voysey   I fear you don't much like Edward.

Mr George Booth (*with pleasant frankness*)   No, I don't.

Mr Voysey   That's a pity. That's a great pity.

Mr George Booth (*with a flattering smile*)   He's not his father and he never will be. What's the time?

Mr Voysey   Twenty past ten.

Mr George Booth   I must be trotting.

As he goes to the door he meets **Edward**, *who comes in apparently looking for his father; at any rate he catches his eye immediately, while* **Mr Booth** *obliviously continues.*

Mr George Booth   I'll look into the drawing room for a second. Stroll home with me?

Mr Voysey   I can't.

Mr George Booth (*mildly surprised at the short reply*)   Well, goodnight. Goodnight, Edward.

He trots away.

Mr Voysey   Leave the table, Phoebe.

Phoebe   Yes, sir.

Mr Voysey   You can come back in ten minutes.

Phoebe *and* **Mary** *depart and the door is closed. Alone with his son,* **Mr Voysey** *does not move. His face grows a little keener, that's all.*

Mr Voysey   Well, Edward?

Edward *starts to move restlessly about, like a cowed animal in a cage; silently for a moment or two. Then when he speaks his voice is toneless, and he does not look at his father.*

Edward Would you mind, sir, dropping with me for the future all these protestations about putting the firm's affairs straight . . . about all your anxieties and sacrifices. I see now, of course . . . a cleverer man than I could have seen it yesterday . . . that for some time, ever since, I suppose, you recovered from the first shock and got used to the double-dealing, this hasn't been your object at all. You've used your clients' capital to produce your own income . . . to bring us up and endow us with. That ten thousand pounds to Booth for his boys; what you're giving Ethel on her marriage . . . It's odd it never struck me yesterday that my own pocket money as a boy must have been drawn from some client's account. I suppose about half the sum you've spent on us first and last would have put things right?

Mr Voysey No, it would not.

Edward (*appealing for the truth*) Come now . . . at some time or other!

Mr Voysey Well, if there have been good times there have been bad. At present the three hundred a year I'm to allow your sister is going to be rather a pull.

Edward Three hundred a year . . . with things as they are! Since it isn't lunacy, sir, I can only conclude that you're enjoying yourself.

Mr Voysey Three trusts . . . two of them big ones . . . have been wound up within this last four years and the accounts have been above suspicion. What's the object of this rodomontade, Edward?

Edward If I'm to remain in the firm it had better be with a very clear understanding of things as they are.

Mr Voysey (*firmly, not too anxiously*) Then you do remain?

Edward (*in a very low voice*) I must remain.

Mr Voysey (*quite gravely*) That's wise of you . . . I'm very glad.

Edward But I make one condition, and I want some information.

Mr Voysey   Well?

Edward   Of course no one has ever discovered . . . and no one suspects this state of things?

Mr Voysey   Peacey knows.

Edward   Peacey!

Mr Voysey   His father found out.

Edward   Oh. Does he draw hush-money?

Mr Voysey (*curling a little at the word*) I have made him a little present from time to time. But I might well have done that in any case. (*He becomes benevolent.*) Peacey's a devoted fellow. I couldn't do without him.

Edward (*with entire comprehension*)   No . . . it would hardly be wise to try. Well . . . the condition I make is a very simple one. It is that we should really try . . . as unobtrusively as you like . . . to put things straight.

Mr Voysey (*with a little polite shrug*)   I've no doubt you'll prove an abler man of business than I have been.

Edward   To begin with we can halve what I draw from the firm.

Mr Voysey   As you please.

Edward   And it seems to me that you can't give Ethel this thousand pounds dowry.

Mr Voysey (*shortly, with one of the quick twists of his eye*)   I have given my word to Denis . . .

Edward   Since the money isn't yours to give.

Mr Voysey (*in an indignant crescendo*)   I should not dream of depriving Ethel of what, as my daughter, she has every right to expect. I am surprised at your suggesting such a thing.

Edward (*pale and firm*)   I am set on this, Father.

Mr Voysey   Don't be such a fool, Edward. What would it look like . . . suddenly refusing without rhyme or reason? What would old Tregoning think?

Edward   Oh, can't you see it's my duty to prevent this?

Mr Voysey   Well . . . you can prevent it . . . by telling the nearest policeman. It is my duty to pay no more attention to such folly than a nurse pays to her child's tantrums. Understand, Edward, I don't want to force you to go on. Come with me gladly, or don't come at all.

Edward (*dully*)   It is my duty to be of what use I can to you, sir. Father, I want to save you if I can.

He flashes into this exclamation of almost broken-hearted affection.
Mr Voysey *looks at his son for a moment and his lip quivers. Then he steels himself.*

Mr Voysey   Thank you! I have been saving myself quite satisfactorily for the last thirty years, and you must please believe that by this time I know my own business best.

Edward (*hopelessly*)   Can't we find the money some other way? How do you manage for your own income?

Mr Voysey   I have a bank balance and a cheque book, haven't I? I spend what I think well to spend. What's the use of earmarking this or that as my own? You say none of it is my own. I might say it's all my own. I think I've earned it.

Edward (*anger coming on him*)   That's what I can't forgive. If you'd lived poor . . . if you'd really done all you could for your clients and not thought of your own pocket . . . then, even though things were no better than they are now . . . why, in a queer sort of way, I could have been proud of you. But, Father, do own the truth . . . I've a right to that from you at least. Didn't you simply seize this chance as a means of money-making?

Mr Voysey (*with a sledgehammer irony*)   Certainly. I sat that morning in my father's office, studying the helmet of the policeman in the street below, and thinking what a glorious path I had happened on to wealth and honour and renown. (*Then he begins to bully* **Edward** *in the kindliest* way.) My dear boy, you don't grasp the ABC of my position. What has carried me to victory? The confidence of my clients. What has earned me that confidence? A decent life, my integrity, my brains?

No, my reputation for wealth that, and nothing else. Business nowadays is run on the lines of the confidence trick. What makes old George Booth so glad to trust me with every penny he possesses? Not affection . . . he's never cared for anything in his life but his collection of French prints.

Edward (*stupefied, helpless*)   Is he involved?

Mr Voysey   Of course he's involved, and he's always after high interest, too . . . it's little one makes out of him. But there's a further question here, Edward. Should I have had confidence in myself, if I'd remained a poor man? No, I should not. In this world you must either be the master of money or its servant. And if one is not opulent in one's daily's life one loses that wonderful . . . financier's touch. One must be confident oneself . . . and I saw from the first that I must at any cost inspire confidence. My whole public and private life has tended to that. All my surroundings . . . you and your brothers and sisters that I have brought into, and up, and put out in the world so worthily . . . you in your turn inspire confidence.

Edward   I sat down yesterday to try and make a list of the people who are good enough to trust their money to us. From George Booth with his money piling up while he sleeps . . . so he fancies . . . to Nursie with her savings, which she brought you so proudly to invest. But you've let those be, at least.

Mr Voysey   Five hundred pounds. I don't know what I did with it.

Edward   But that's damnable.

Mr Voysey   Indeed? I give her seventy-five pounds a year for it. Would you like to take charge of that account, Edward? I'll give you five hundred to invest tomorrow.

Edward, *hopelessly beaten, falls into an almost comic state of despair.*

Edward   My dear Father, putting every moral question aside . . . it's all very well your playing Robin Hood in this magnificent manner; but have you given a moment's thought to the sort of inheritance you'll be leaving me?

Mr Voysey (*pleased for the first time*)   Ah! that's a question you have every right to ask.

Edward   If you died tomorrow could we pay eight shillings in the pound . . . or seventeen . . . or five? Do you k n o w ?

Mr Voysey   And the answer is, that by your help I have every intention, when I die, of leaving a personal estate that will run into six figures. D'you think I've given my life and my talents for a less result than that? I'm fond of you all and I want you to be proud of me . . . and I mean that the name of Voysey shall be carried high in the world by my children and grandchildren. Don't you be afraid, Edward. Ah, you lack experience, my boy . . . you're not full-grown yet . . . your impulses are a bit chaotic. You emotionalise over your work, and you reason about your emotions. You must sort yourself. You must realise that money-making is one thing, and religion another, and family life a third . . . and that if we apply our energies wholeheartedly to each of these in turn, and realise that different laws govern each, that there is a different end to be served, a different ideal to be striven for in each . . .

His coherence is saved by the sudden appearance of his wife, who comes round the door smiling benignly. Not in the least put out, in fact a little relieved, he greets her with an affectionate shout, for she is very deaf.

Mr Voysey   Hullo, Mother!

Mrs Voysey   Oh, there you are, Trench. I've been deserted.

Mr Voysey   George Booth gone?

Mrs Voysey   Are you talking business? Perhaps you don't want me.

Mr Voysey   No, no . . . no business.

Mrs Voysey (*who has not looked for his answer*)   I suppose the others are in the billiard room.

Mr Voysey (*vociferously*)   We're not talking business, old lady.

Edward   I'll be off, sir.

Mr Voysey (*genial as usual*)   Why don't you stay? I'll come up with you in the morning.

Edward   No, thank you, sir.

Mr Voysey   Then I'll be up about noon.

Edward   Goodnight, Mother.

Mrs Voysey *places a plump, kindly hand on his arm and looks up affectionately.*

Mrs Voysey   You look tired.

Edward   No, I'm not.

Mrs Voysey   What did you say?

Edward (*too weary to repeat himself*)   Nothing, Mother dear.

He kisses her cheek, while she kisses the air.

Mr Voysey   Goodnight, my boy.

Then he goes. **Mrs Voysey** *is carrying her* Notes and Queries. *This is a dear old lady, looking older too than probably she is. Placid describes her. She has had a life of little joys and cares, has never measured herself against the world, never even questioned the shape and size of the little corner of it in which she lives. She has loved an indulgent husband and borne eight children, six of them surviving, healthy. That is her history.*

Mrs Voysey   George Booth went some time ago. He said he thought you'd taken a chill walking round the garden.

Mr Voysey   I'm all right.

Mrs Voysey   D'you think you have?

Mr Voysey (*in her ear*)   No.

Mrs Voysey   You should be careful, Trench. What did you put on?

Mr Voysey   Nothing.

Mrs Voysey   How very foolish! Let me feel your hand. You are quite feverish.

Mr Voysey (*affectionately*)   You're a fuss-box, old lady.

Mrs Voysey (*coquetting with him*)   Don't be rude, Trench.

Honor *descends upon them, She is well into that nightly turmoil of putting everything and everybody to rights which always precedes her bedtime. She carries a shawl, which she claps round her mother's shoulders, her mind and gaze already on the next thing to be done.*

Honor   Mother, you left your shawl in the drawing room. Oh . . . can't they finish clearing?

Mr Voysey (*arranging the folds of the shawl with real tenderness*) Now who's careless!

Phoebe *comes into the room.*

Honor   Phoebe, finish here and then you must bring in the tray for Mr Hugh.

Mrs Voysey (*having looked at the shawl and **Honor**, and connected the matter in her mind*)   Thank you, Honor. You'd better look after your father; he's been walking round the garden without his cape.

Honor   Papa!

Mr Voysey   Phoebe, you get that little kettle and boil it, and brew me some whisky and water. I shall be all right.

Honor (*fluttering more than ever*)   I'll get it. Where's the whisky? And Hugh coming back at ten o'clock with no dinner. No wonder his work goes wrong. Here it is! Papa, you do d e s e r v e to be ill.

Clasping the whisky decanter she is off again. **Mrs Voysey** *sits at the dinner table and adjusts her spectacles. She returns to* Notes and Queries, *one elbow firmly planted and her plump hand against her plump cheek. This is her favourite attitude; and she is apt, when reading, to soliloquise in her deaf woman's voice. At least, whether she considers it soliloquy or conversation is not easy to discover.* **Mr Voysey** *stands with his back to the fire, grumbling and pulling faces.*

Mrs Voysey   This is a very perplexing correspondence about the Cromwell family. One can't deny the man had good

blood in him . . . his grandfather Sir Henry, his uncle Sir
Oliver . . .

Mr Voysey   There's a pain in my back.

Mrs Voysey   . . . and it's difficult to discover where the taint
crept in.

Mr Voysey   I believe I strained myself putting in those
strawberry plants.

Mary, *the house-parlourmaid, carries in a tray of warned-up dinner for*
Hugh *and plants it on the table.*

Mrs Voysey   Yes, but then how was it he came to disgrace
himself so? I believe the family disappeared. Regicide is a root
and branch curse. You must read the letter signed CWA . . .
it's quite interesting. There's a misprint in mine about the first
umbrella-maker . . . now where was it . . .

And so the dear lady will ramble on indefinitely.

Act Three

The dining room looks very different in the white light of a July noon. Moreover, on this particular day, it isn't even its normal self. There is a peculiar luncheon spread on the table and on it are decanters of port and sherry; sandwiches, biscuits and an uncut cake; two little piles of plates and one little pile of napkins. There are no table decorations, and indeed the whole room has been made as bare and as tidy as possible. Such preparations denote one of the recognised English festivities, and the appearance of **Phoebe**, *the maid, who has just completed them, the set solemnity of her face and the added touches of black to her dress and cap, suggest that this is probably a funeral. When* **Mary** *comes in, the fact that she has evidently been crying and that she decorously does not raise her voice above an unpleasant whisper makes it quite certain.*

Mary   Phoebe, they're coming back . . . and I forgot one of the blinds in the drawing-room.

Phoebe   Well, pull it up quick and make yourself scarce, I'll open the door.

Mary *got rid of,* **Phoebe** *composes her face still more rigorously into the aspect of formal grief and with a touch to her apron as well goes to admit the funeral party. The first to enter are* **Mrs Voysey** *and* **Mr Booth**, *she on his arm; and the fact that she is in widow's weeds makes the occasion clear. The little old man leads his old friend very tenderly.*

Mr George Booth   Will you come in here?

Mrs Voysey   Thank you.

With great solicitude he puts her in a chair; then takes her hand.

Mr George Booth   Now I'll intrude no longer.

Mrs Voysey   You'll take some lunch?

Mr George Booth   No.

Mrs Voysey   Not a glass of wine?

Mr George Booth   If there's anything I can do just send round.

Mrs Voysey Thank you.

He reaches the door only to be met by the **Major** *and his wife. He shakes hands with them both.*

Mr George Booth My dear Emily! My dear Booth!

Emily *is a homely, patient, pale little woman of about thirty-five. She looks smaller that usual in her heavy black dress and is meeker than usual on an occasion of this kind. The* **Major**, *on the other hand, though his grief is most sincere, has an irresistible air of being responsible for, and indeed rather proud of, the whole affair.*

Major Booth Voysey I think it all went off as he would have wished.

Mr George Booth (*feeling that he is called on for praise*) Great credit . . . great credit.

He makes another attempt to escape and is stopped this time by **Trenchard Voysey**, *to whom he is extending a hand and beginning his formula. But* **Trenchard** *speaks first.*

Trenchard Have you the right time?

Mr George Booth (*taken aback and fumbling for this watch*) I think so . . . I make it fourteen minutes to one. (*He seizes the occasion.*) Trenchard, as a very old and dear friend of your father's, you won't mind me saying how glad I was that you were present today. Death closes all. Indeed it must be a great regret to you that you did not see him before . . . before . . .

Trenchard (*his cold eye freezing this little gush*) I don't think he asked for me.

Mr George Booth (*stoppered*) No? No! Well . . . well . . .

At this third attempt to depart he actually collides with someone in the doorway. It is **Hugh Voysey**.

Mr George Booth My dear Hugh . . . I won't intrude.

Determined to escape, he grasps his hand, gasps out his formula and is off. **Trenchard** *and* **Hugh**, *eldest and youngest son, are as unlike each other as it is possible for Voyseys to be, but that isn't very unlike.*

Trenchard *has the cocksure manner of the successful barrister;* **Hugh** *the sweetly querulous air of diffidence and scepticism belonging to the unsuccessful man of letters or artist. The self-respect of* **Trenchard***'s appearance is immense, and he cultivates that air of concentration upon any trivial matter, or even upon nothing at all, which will some day make him an impressive figure upon the Bench.* **Hugh** *is always vague, searching Heaven or the corners of the room for inspiration; and even on this occasion his tie is abominably crooked. The inspissated gloom of this assembly, to which each member of the family as he arrives adds his share, is unbelievable.* **Hugh** *is depressed partly at the inadequacy of his grief;* **Trenchard** *conscientiously preserves an air of the indifference which he feels; the* **Major** *stands statuesque at the mantelpiece; while* **Emily** *is by* **Mrs Voysey***, whose face in its quiet grief is nevertheless a mirror of many happy memories of her husband.*

Major Booth Voysey   I wouldn't hang over her, Emily.

Emily   No, of course not.

Apologetically she sits by the table.

Trenchard   I hope your wife is well, Hugh?

Hugh   Thank you, Trench: I think so. Beatrice is in America . . . giving some lectures there.

Trenchard   Really!

Then comes in a small, well-groomed, bullet-headed schoolboy. This is the **Major***'s eldest son. Looking scared and solemn, he goes straight to his mother.*

Emily   Now be very quiet, Christopher.

Then **Denis Tregoning** *appears.*

Trenchard   Oh, Tregoning, did you bring Honor back?

Denis   Yes.

Major Booth Voysey (*at the table*)   A glass of wine, Mother?

Mrs Voysey   What?

The **Major** *hardly knows how to turn his whisper decorously into enough of a shout for his mother to hear. But he manages it.*

Major Booth Voysey   Have a glass of wine?

Mrs Voysey   Sherry, please.

While he pours it out with an air of its being medicine on this occasion and not wine at all, **Edward** *comes quickly into the room, his face very set, his mind obviously on other matters than the funeral. No one speaks to him for the moment and he has time to observe them all.* **Trenchard** *is continuing his talk to* **Denis**.

Trenchard   Give my love to Ethel. Is she ill that . . .

Tregoning   Not exactly, but she couldn't very well be with us. I thought perhaps you might have heard. We're expecting . . . (*He hesitates with the bashfulness of a young husband.*)

Trenchard   Indeed. I congratulate you. I hope all will be well. Please give my best love to Ethel.

Major Booth Voysey (*in an awful voice*)   Lunch, Emily?

Emily (*scared*)   I suppose so, Booth, thank you.

Major Booth Voysey   I think the boy had better run away and play . . . (*He checks himself on the word.*) Well, take a book and keep quiet; d'ye hear me, Christopher?

Christopher, *who looks incapable of a sound, gazes at his father with round eyes.* **Emily** *whispers 'Library' to him and adds a kiss in acknowledgement of his good behaviour. After a moment he slips out, thankfully.*

Edward   How's Ethel, Denis?

Tregoning   A little smashed, of course, but no harm done I hope. The doctor's a bit worried about her, though.

Alice Maitland *comes in, brisk and businesslike; a little impatient of this universal cloud of mourning.*

Alice   Edward, Honor has gone to her room; I must take her some food and make her eat it. She's very upset.

Edward   Make her drink a glass of wine, and say it is necessary she should come down here. And d'you mind not coming back yourself, Alice?

Alice (*her eyebrows up*)   Certainly, if you wish.

Major Booth Voysey (*overhearing*)   What's this? What's this?

Alice *gets her glass of wine and goes. The* **Major** *is suddenly full of importance.*

Major Booth Voysey   What is this, Edward?

Edward   I have something to say to you all.

Major Booth Voysey   What?

Edward   Well, Booth, you'll hear when I say it.

Major Booth Voysey   Is it business? . . . because I think this is scarcely the time for business.

Edward   Why?

Major Booth Voysey   Do you find it easy to descend from your natural grief to the consideration of money? . . . I do not. (*He finds* **Trenchard** *at his elbow.*) I hope you are getting some lunch, Trenchard.

Edward   This is business and rather more than business, Booth. I choose now, because it is something I wish to say to the family, not write to each individually . . . and it will be difficult to get us all together again.

Major Booth Voysey (*determined at any rate to give his sanction*) Well, Trenchard, as Edward is in the position of trustee . . . executor . . . I don't know your terms . . . I suppose . . .

Trenchard   I don't see what your objection is.

Major Booth Voysey (*with some superiority*)   Don't you? I should not call myself a sentimental man, but . . .

Edward   You had better stay, Denis; you represent Ethel.

Tregoning (*who has not heard the beginning of this*)   Why?

Honor *has obediently come down from her room. She is pale and thin, shaken with grief and worn out besides; for, needless to say, the brunt of her father's illness, the brunt of everything, has been on her. Six weeks' nursing, part of it hopeless, will exhaust anyone. Her handkerchief is to* *her eyes, and every minute or two they flood over with tears.* **Edward** *goes and affectionately puts his arm round her.*

Edward   My dear Honor, I am sorry to be so . . . so merciless. There! . . . there!

He hands her into the room; then turns and once more surveys the family, who this time mostly return the compliment. Then he says shortly.

I think you might all sit down. (*And then, since the* **Major** *happens to be conveniently near . . .*) Shut the door, Booth.

Major Booth Voysey   Shut the door!

But he does so, with as much dignity as possible. **Edward** *goes close to his mother and speaks very distinctly, very kindly.*

Edward   Mother, we're all going to have a little necessary talk over matters . . . now, because it's most convenient. I hope it won't . . . I hope you won't mind. Will you come to the table?

Mrs Voysey *looks up as if understanding more than he says.*

Mrs Voysey   Edward . . .

Edward   Yes, Mother dear?

Major Booth Voysey (*commandingly*)   You'll sit here, Mother, of course.

He places her in her accustomed chair at the foot of the table. One by one the others sit down, **Edward** *apparently last. But then he discovers that* **Hugh** *has lost himself in a corner of the room and is gazing into vacancy.*

Edward (*with a touch of kindly exasperation*)   Hugh, would you mind attending?

Hugh   What is it?

Edward   There's a chair.

Hugh *takes it. Then for a moment – while* **Edward** *is trying to frame in coherent sentences what he must say to them – for a minute there is silence, broken only by* **Honor***'s sniffs, which culminate at last in a noisy little cascade of tears.*

Major Booth Voysey   Honor, control yourself.

And to emphasise his own perfect control he helps himself majestically to a glass of sherry. Then says . . .

Major Booth Voysey   Well, Edward?

Edward   I'll come straight to the point which concerns you. Our father's will gives certain sums to you all . . . the gross amount would be something over a hundred thousand pounds. There will be no money.

He can get no further than the bare statement, which is received only with varying looks of bewilderment; until **Mrs Voysey**, *discovering nothing from their faces, breaks this second silence.*

Mrs Voysey   I didn't hear.

Hugh (*in his mother's ear*)   Edward says there's no money.

Trenchard (*precisely*)   I think you said . . . 'will be'.

Major Booth Voysey (*in a tone of mitigated thunder*)   Why will there be no money?

Edward (*letting himself go*)   Because every penny by right belongs to the clients, Father spent his life in defrauding. I mean that in its worst sense . . . swindling . . . thieving. And now I must collect every penny, any money that you can give me; put the firm into bankruptcy; pay back all we can. I'll stand my trial . . . it'll come to that with me . . . and the sooner the better. (*He pauses, partly for breath, and glares at them all.*) Are none of you going to speak? Quite right, what is there to be said? (*Then with a gentle afterthought.*) I'm sorry to hurt you, Mother.

The Voysey family seems buried deep beneath this avalanche of horror. All but **Mrs Voysey**, *who has been watching* **Edward** *closely, and now says very calmly.*

Mrs Voysey   I can't hear quite all you say, but I guess what it is. You don't hurt me, Edward . . . I have known of this for a long time.

Edward (*with a muted cry*)   Oh Mother, did he know you knew?

Mrs Voysey   What do you say?

Trenchard (*collected and dry*)   I may as well tell you, Edward; I suspected everything wasn't right about the time of my last quarrel with my father. As there was nothing I could do I did not pursue my suspicions. Was Father aware that you knew, Mother?

Mrs Voysey   We never discussed it. There was once a great danger, I believe . . . when you were all younger . . . of his being found out. But we never discussed it.

Edward (*swallowing a fresh bitterness*)   I'm glad it isn't such a shock to all of you.

Hugh (*alive to the dramatic aspect of the matter*)   My God . . . before the earth has settled on his grave!

Edward   I thought it wrong to put off telling you.

Honor, *the word 'swindling' having spelt itself out in her mind, at last gives way to a burst of piteous grief.*

Honor   Oh poor Papa! . . . poor Papa!

Edward (*comforting her kindly*)   Honor, we shall want your help and advice.

The **Major** *has recovered from the shock, to swell with importance. It being necessary to make an impression, he instinctively turns first to his wife.*

Major Booth Voysey   I think, Emily, there was no need for you to be present at this exposure, and that now you had better retire.

Emily   Very well, Booth.

She gets up to go, conscious of her misdemeanour. But as she reaches the door, an awful thought strikes the **Major**.

Major Booth Voysey   Good Heavens . . . I hope the servants haven't been listening! See where they are, Emily . . . and keep them away . . distract them. Open the door suddenly.

She does so, more or less, and there is no one behind it.

That's all right.

Having watched his wife's departure, he turns with gravity to his brother.

I have said nothing as yet, Edward. I am thinking.

Trenchard (*a little impatient at this exhibition*)   That's the worst of these family practices . . . a lot of money knocking around and no audit ever required. The wonder to me is to find an honest solicitor of that sort anywhere.

Major Booth Voysey   Really, Trenchard!

Trenchard   Well, think of the temptation.

Edward   And most people are such innocents . . .

Trenchard   Of course the whole world is getting more and more into the hands of its experts . . .

Edward   Here were these funds . . . a kind of lucky bag into which he dipped.

Trenchard   But he must have kept accounts of some sort.

Edward   Scraps of paper. The separate funds . . . most of them I can't even trace. The capital doesn't exist.

Major Booth Voysey   Where's it gone?

Edward (*very directly*)   You've been living on it.

Major Booth Voysey   Good God!

Trenchard   What can you pay in the pound?

Edward   As we stand? . . . six or seven shillings, I daresay. But we must do better than that.

To which there is no response.

Major Booth Voysey   All this is very dreadful. Does it mean beggary for the whole family?

Edward   Yes, it should.

Trenchard (*sharply*)   Nonsense.

Edward (*joining issue at once*)　What right have we to a thing we possess?

Trenchard　He didn't make you an allowance, Booth? Your capital's your own, isn't it?

Major Booth Voysey (*awkwardly placed between the two of them*) Really . . . I . . . I suppose so.

Trenchard　How long have you had it?

Major Booth Voysey　Oh . . . when I married . . .

Trenchard　Then that's all right.

Edward (*vehemently*)　It was stolen money . . . it must have been.

Trenchard　Possibly . . . but possibly not. And Booth took it in good faith.

Major Booth Voysey　I should hope so!

Edward (*dwelling on the words*)　It's stolen money.

Major Booth Voysey (*bubbling with distress*)　I say, what ought I to do?

Trenchard　Do . . . my dear Booth? Nothing.

Edward (*with great indignation*)　Trenchard, we owe reparation.

Trenchard　No doubt. But to whom? From which client's account was Booth's money taken? You say yourself you don't know.

Edward (*grieved*)　Trenchard!

Trenchard　My dear Edward . . . the law will take anything it has a right to and all it can get; you needn't be afraid. But what about y o u r position . . . can we get you clear?

Edward　Oh . . . I'll face the music.

The **Major** *'s head has been turning incessantly from one to the other and by this he is just a bristle of alarm.*

Major Booth Voysey   But I say, you know, this is awful!
Will the thing have to be made public?

Trenchard   No help for it.

*The **Major***'s jaw drops; he is speechless. **Mrs Voysey**'s dead voice
steals in.

Mrs Voysey   What is all this?

Trenchard   I am explaining, Mother, that the family is not
called upon to beggar itself in order to pay back to every client
to whom Father owed a pound perhaps eight shillings instead
of seven.

Mrs Voysey   He will find that my estate has been kept
separate.

Trenchard   I'm very glad to hear it, Mother.

Edward *hides his face in his hands.*

Mrs Voysey   When Mr Barnes died, your father agreed to
appointing another trustee.

Tregoning (*diffidently*)   I suppose, Edward, I'm involved?

Edward (*lifting his head quickly*)   Denis, I hope not. I didn't
know that anything of yours . . .

Tregoning   Yes . . . all I got under my aunt's will.

Edward   See how things are . . . I've not found a trace of
that yet. We'll hope for the best.

Tregoning (*setting his teeth*)   It can't be helped.

*The **Major** leans over the table and speaks in the loudest of whispers.*

Major Booth Voysey   Let me advise you to say nothing of
this to Ethel at such a critical time.

Tregoning   Thank you, Booth . . . naturally I shan't.

Hugh, *by a series of contortions, has lately been giving evidence of a
desire or intention to say something.*

Edward   Well, what is it, Hugh?

Hugh　I have been wondering . . . if he can hear this conversation.

Up to now it has all been meaningless to **Honor**, *in her nervous dilapidation; but this remark brings a fresh burst of tears.*

Honor　Oh, poor Papa . . . poor Papa!

Mrs Voysey　I think I'll go to my room. I can't hear what any of you are saying. Edward can tell me afterwards.

Edward　Would you like to go too, Honor?

Honor (*through her sobs*)　Yes, please, I would.

Tregoning　I'll get out, Edward. Whatever you think fit to do . . . ! I'm on one side of the fence and Ethel's on the other, so to speak. I wish I'd more work on hand . . . for her sake . . . and the child's. That's all.

By this time **Mrs Voysey** *and* **Honor** *have been got out of the room.* **Tregoning** *follows them, and the four brothers are left together.* **Hugh** *is vacant,* **Edward** *does not speak,* **Booth** *looks at* **Trenchard**, *who settles himself to acquire information.*

Trenchard　How long have things been wrong?

Edward　He told me the trouble began in his father's time and that he'd been battling with it ever since.

Trenchard (*smiling*)　Oh, come now . . . that's hardly possible.

Edward　I believed him. Of course, I've barely begun on the papers yet. But I doubt if I'll be able to trace anything more than twenty years back . . . unless it's to do with old George Booth's business.

Major Booth Voysey　But the Pater never touched his money . . . why, he was a personal friend.

Trenchard　How long now since he told you?

Edward　Last autumn.

Trenchard　What has been happening since?

Edward　He got ill in November . . . which didn't make him any easier to deal with. I began by trying to make him put some of the smaller people right. He said that was penny wise and pound foolish. So I've been doing what I could myself this last month or so. Oh . . . nothing to count.

Trenchard   He didn't think you'd actually take a hand?

Edward   First it was that he was in a corner and I was to help him out. Then we were to clean up the whole mess and have a quarter of a million to the good. That was in February . . . when the new Kaffir boom was on.

Trenchard   He was in that, was he?

Edward   Up to the neck. And I believe he'd have made a pile if he hadn't been ill. As it was, he got out fifteen thousand to the good.

Major Booth Voysey   Really!

Edward   I'm not sure he didn't only tell me because he wanted someone to boast to about his financial exploits.

Trenchard   Got more reckless as he got older, I suppose.

Edward   Oh . . . mere facts meant nothing to him. He drew up this will in May. He knew then he'd nothing to leave . . . on the balance. But there it all is . . . legacies to servants . . . and charities. And I'm the sole executor . . . with an extra thousand for my trouble!

Trenchard   Childish! Was I down for anything?

Edward   No.

Trenchard (*without resentment*)   How he did hate me!

Edward   You're spared the results of his affection anyway.

Trenchard   What on earth made you stay with him once you knew?

Edward *does not answer for a moment.*

Edward   I thought I might prevent things getting worse.

Trenchard   I'm afraid your position . . . at the best . . . is not a pleasant one.

Edward (*bowing his head*)   I know.

Trenchard, *the only one of the three who comprehends, looks at his brother for a moment with something that might almost be admiration. Then he stirs himself.*

Trenchard   I must be off. Work waiting . . . end of term.

Major Booth Voysey   Shall I walk to the station with you?

Trenchard   I'll spend a few minutes with Mother. (*He says, at the door, very respectfully.*) You'll count on me for any professional help I can give, please, Edward.

Edward (*simply*)   Thank you, Trenchard.

So **Trenchard** *goes. And the* **Major**, *who has been endeavouring to fathom his final attitude, then comments:*

Major Booth Voysey   No heart, y'know! Great brain! If it hadn't been for that distressing quarrel, he might have saved our poor father. Don't you think so, Edward?

Edward   Perhaps.

Hugh (*giving vent to his thoughts at last with something of a relish*) The more I think this out, the more devilishly humorous it gets. Old Booth breaking down by the grave . . . Colpus reading the service . . .

Edward   Yes, the Vicar's badly hit.

Hugh   Oh, the Pater had managed his business for years.

Major Booth Voysey   Good God . . . how shall we ever look old Booth in the face again?

Edward   I don't worry about him; he can die quite comfortably enough on our six shillings in the pound. It's one or two of the smaller fry who will suffer.

Major Booth Voysey   Now, just explain to me . . . I didn't interrupt while Trenchard was speaking . . . of what exactly did this defrauding consist?

Edward   Speculating with a client's capital. You pocket the gains . . . and you keep paying the client his ordinary income.

Major Booth Voysey   So that he doesn't find out?

Edward   Quite so.

Major Booth Voysey   In point of fact, he doesn't suffer?

Edward   He doesn't suffer till he finds it out.

Major Booth Voysey   And all that's wrong now is that some of their capital is missing.

Edward (*half-amused, half-amazed at this process of reasoning*)   Yes, that's all that's wrong.

Major Booth Voysey   What is the − ah − deficit? (*The word rolls from his tongue.*)

Edward   Anything between two and three hundred thousand pounds.

Major Booth Voysey (*impressed, and not unfavourably*)   Dear me . . . this is a big affair!

Hugh (*following his own line of thought*)   Quite apart from the rights and wrongs of this, only a very able man could have kept a straight face to the world all these years, as the Pater did.

Major Booth Voysey   But he often made money by these speculations?

Edward   Very often. His own expenditure was heavy . . . as y o u know.

Major Booth Voysey (*with gratitude for favours received*)   He was a very generous man.

Hugh   Did nobody ever suspect?

Edward   You see, Hugh, when there was any pressing danger . . . if a trust had to be wound up . . . he'd make a great effort and put the accounts straight.

Major Booth Voysey   Then he did put some accounts straight?

Edward   Yes, when he couldn't help himself.

The **Major** *looks very inquiring, and then squares himself up to the subject.*

Major Booth Voysey   Now look here, Edward. You told us that he told you that it was the object of his life to put these accounts straight. Then you laughed at that. Now you tell me that he did put some accounts straight.

Edward (*wearily*)   My dear Booth, you don't understand.

Major Booth Voysey   Well, let me understand . . . I am anxious to understand.

Edward   We can't pay ten shillings in the pound.

Major Booth Voysey   That's very dreadful. But do you know that there wasn't a time when we couldn't have paid five?

Edward (*acquiescent*)   Perhaps.

Major Booth Voysey   Very well, then! If it was true about his father and all that . . . and why shouldn't we believe him if we can? . . . and he did effect an improvement, that's to his credit, isn't it? Let us at least be just, Edward.

Edward (*patiently polite*)   I am sorry if I seem unjust. But he has left me in a rather unfortunate position.

Major Booth Voysey   Yes, his death was a tragedy. It seems to me that if he had been spared he might have succeeded at length in this tremendous task and restored to us our family honour.

Edward   Yes, Booth, he sometimes spoke very feelingly of that.

Major Booth Voysey (*irony lost upon him*)   I can well believe it. And I can tell you that now . . . I may be right or I may be wrong . . . I am feeling far less concerned about the clients' money than I am at the terrible blow to the family which this exposure will strike. Money, after all, can to a certain extent be done without . . . but honour . . .

This is too much for **Edward**.

Edward   Our honour! Does any one of you mean to give me a single penny towards undoing all the wrong that has been done?

Major Booth Voysey   I take Trenchard's word for it that that . . . is quite unnecessary.

Edward   Then don't talk to me about honour.

Major Booth Voysey (*somewhat nettled at this outburst*)   I am thinking of the public exposure. Edward, can't that be prevented?

Edward (*with quick suspicion*)   How?

Major Booth Voysey   Well, how was it being prevented before he died . . . before we knew anything about it?

Edward (*appealing to the spirits that watch over him*)   Oh, listen to this! First Trenchard . . . and now you! You've the poison in your blood, every one of you. Who am I to talk! I daresay so have I.

Major Booth Voysey (*reprovingly*)   I am beginning to think that you have worked yourself into rather an hysterical state over this unhappy business.

Edward (*rating him*)   Perhaps you'd have been glad . . . glad if I'd gone on lying and cheating . . . and married and begotten a son to go on lying and cheating after me . . . and to pay you your interest in the lie and the cheat.

Major Booth Voysey (*with statesmanlike calm*)   Look here, Edward, this rhetoric is exceedingly out of place. The simple question before us is . . . what is the best course to pursue?

Edward   There is no question before us. There's only one course to pursue.

Major Booth Voysey (*crushingly*)   You will let me speak, please. In so far as our poor father was dishonest to his clients, I pray that he may be forgiven. In so far as he spent his life honestly endeavouring to right a wrong which he had found already committed . . . I forgive him . . . I admire him,

Edward . . . and I feel it my duty to – er – reprobate most strongly the – er – gusto with which you have been holding him up in memory to us . . . ten minutes after we'd been standing round his grave . . . as a monster of wickedness. I think I knew him as well as you . . . better. And . . . thank God! . . . there was not between him and me this . . . this unhappy business to warp my judgment of him. (*He warms to his subject.*) Did you ever know a more charitable man . . . a larger-hearted? He was a faithful husband . . . and what a father to all of us! . . . putting us out into the world and fully intending to leave us comfortably settled there. Further . . . as I see this matter, Edward . . . when as a young man he was told this terrible secret and entrusted with such a frightful task . . . did he turn his back on it like a coward? No. He went through it heroically to the end of his life. And, as he died, I imagine there was no more torturing thought than that he had left his work unfinished. (*He is pleased with this peroration.*) And now . . . if all these clients can be kept receiving their natural incomes and if father's plan could be carried out, of gradually replacing the capital . . .

Edward *at this raises his head and stares with horror.*

Edward   You're asking me to carry on this . . . ? Oh, you don't know what you're talking about.

The **Major**, *having talked himself back to a proper eminence, remains good tempered.*

Major Booth Voysey   Well, I'm not a conceited man . . . but I do think that I can understand a simple financial problem when it has been explained to me.

Edward   You don't know the nerve . . . the unscrupulous daring it requires to . . .

Major Booth Voysey   Of course, if you're going to argue round your own incompetence.

Edward (*very straight*)   D'you want your legacy?

Major Booth Voysey (*with dignity*)   In one moment I shall get very angry. Here am I doing my best to help you and your clients . . . and there you sit imputing to me the most sordid motives. Do you suppose I should touch, or allow to be touched, the money which father has left us till every client's claim was satisfied?

Edward   My dear Booth, I know you mean well . . .

Major Booth Voysey   I'll come down to your office and work with you.

At this cheerful prospect even poor **Edward** *can't help smiling.*

Edward   I'm sure you would.

Major Booth Voysey (*feeling that it is a chance lost*)   If the Pater had ever consulted me . . .

At this point **Trenchard** *looks round the door to say . . .*

Trenchard   Are you coming, Booth?

Major Booth Voysey   Yes, certainly. I'll talk this over with Trenchard. (*As he gets up and automatically stiffens, he is reminded of the occasion and his voice drops.*) I say . . . we've been speaking very loud. You must do nothing rash. I've no doubt he and I can devise something which will obviate . . . and then I'm sure I shall convince you . . . (*Glancing into the hall he apparently catches his eldest brother's impatient eye, for he departs abruptly, saying . . .*) All right, Trenchard, you've eight minutes.

The **Major**'s *departure leaves* **Hugh**, *at any rate, really at his ease.*

Hugh   This is an experience for you, Edward!

Edward (*bitterly*)   And I feared what the shock might be to you all! Booth has made a good recovery.

Hugh   You wouldn't have him miss such a chance of booming at us.

Edward   It's strange that people will believe you can do right by means which they know to be wrong.

Hugh (*taking great interest in this*)   Come, what do we know about right and wrong? Let's say legal and illegal. You're so down on the governor because he has trespassed against the etiquette of your own profession. But now he's dead . . . and if there weren't any scandal to think of . . . it's no use the rest of us pretending to feel him a criminal. Because we don't. Which just shows that money . . . and property . . .

*At this point he becomes conscious that **Alice Maitland** is standing behind him, her eyes fixed on his brother. So he interrupts himself to ask . . .*

Hugh   D'you want to speak to Edward?

Alice   Please, Hugh.

Hugh   I'll go.

*He goes, a little martyr-like, to conclude the evolution of his theory in soliloquy. His usual fate. **Alice** still looks at **Edward**, and he at her rather appealingly.*

Alice   Auntie has told me.

Edward   He was fond of you. Don't think worse of him than you can help.

Alice   I'm thinking of you.

Edward   I may just escape.

Alice   So Trenchard says.

Edward   My hands are clean, Alice.

Alice   I know that.

Edward   Mother's not very upset.

Alice   She'd expected a smash in his lifetime.

Edward   I'm glad that didn't happen.

Alice   Yes. I've put Honor to bed. It was a mercy to tell her just at this moment. She can grieve for his death and his disgrace at the same time . . . and the one grief will soften the other perhaps.

Edward   Oh, they're all shocked enough at the disgrace . . . but will they open their purses to lessen the disgrace?

Alice   Will it seem less disgraceful to have stolen ten thousand pounds than twenty?

Edward   I should think so.

Alice   I should think so, but I wonder if that's the law. If it isn't, Trenchard wouldn't consider the point. I'm sure public opinion doesn't say so . . . and that's what Booth is considering.

Edward (*with contempt*)   Yes.

Alice (*ever so gently ironical*)   Well, he's in the Army . . . he's almost in society . . . and he has got to get on in both; one mustn't blame him.

Edward (*very serious*)   But when one thinks how the money was obtained!

Alice   When one thinks how most money is obtained!

Edward   They've not e a r n e d it.

Alice (*her eyes humorous*)   If they had they might have given it you and earned more. Did I ever tell you what my guardian said to me when I came of age?

Edward   I'm thankful you're out of the mess.

Alice   I shouldn't have been, but I was made to look after my affairs myself . . . much against my will. My guardian was a person of great character and no principles, the best and most lovable man I've ever met . . . I'm sorry you never knew him, Edward . . . and he said once to me: 'You've no moral right to your money . . . you've not earned it or deserved it in any way. So don't be either surprised or annoyed when any enterprising person tries to get it from you. He has at least as much moral right to it as you . . . if he can use it better perhaps he has more.' Shocking sentiments, aren't they? But perhaps that's why I've less pity for some of these clients than you have, Edward.

Edward *shakes his head, treating these paradoxes as they deserve.*

Edward   Alice . . . one or two of them will be beggared.

Alice (*sincerely*)   Yes, that is bad. What's to be done?

Edward   There's old Nurse . . . with her poor little savings gone!

Alice   Something can be done for her . . . surely.

Edward   The law's no respecter of persons . . . that's its boast. Old Booth with more than he wants will keep enough and to spare. My old Nurse, with just enough, may starve. But it'll be a relief to clear out this nest of lies, even though one suffers one's self. I've been ashamed to walk into that office, I'll hold my head high in prison though.

He shakes himself stiffly erect, his chin high. **Alice** *quizzes him.*

Alice   Edward, I'm afraid you're feeling heroic.

Edward   I!

Alice   You looked quite like Booth for the moment. (*This effectually removes the starch.*) Please don't glory in your martyrdom. It will be very stupid to send you to prison, and you must do your very best to keep out. (*Her tone is most practical.*) We were talking about these people who'll be beggared.

Edward (*simply*)   I didn't mean to be heroic.

Alice   I know. But there's the danger in acting on principle one begins to think more of one's attitude than of the use of what one is doing.

Edward   But I've no choice in the matter. There's only the one thing I can do.

Alice   Run the ship ashore? Well . . . if you say so!

Edward   Unless you expect me to t a k e Booth's advice . . . turn honest cheat . . . juggle and speculate in the hope that . . . Oh, my dear Alice . . . no! If it were only a question of a few thousands . . . ! But I'm no good at that sort of thing anyway. It'd simply make matters worse. I've been sitting down . . . self-pityingly . . . under the shame of it all these months. I did . . . take a hand . . . and stop one affair going from bad to worse. I'd no right to. Sheer favouritism! I shall suffer for it now.

Alice   That's nobody's business but your own.

Edward   I could go on doing that . . . putting the worst cases straight . . . say for a year . . . or till I'm found out, as I almost certainly should be. For don't think I'd be any good at the game, Alice. (*Then his tone changes; he is glancing inward.*) But you know . . . there's something in me that'd rather like to try. (*He looks her full in the face.*) What do you say?

Alice (*catching her breath*)   Dear Edward . . . I can't advise.

Edward (*with grimly whimsical humour*)   You've undermined my principles. I must have some help in exchange.

Alice   I'm lawless at heart, I fear. Most women are. What would happen at the end of the year?

Edward   Then I should have to do what I ought to do now . . . send round a polite letter: 'Dear Sir or Madam . . . I am a thief . . . please call the police. For I can't succeed. Understand that. I can't make up a quarter of a million by careful management.

Alice   Will it be much worse for you . . . if at last they do call the police?

Edward   That . . . as you said . . . would be nobody's business but my own.

Alice   I'd do anything to help you . . . anything. That sounds like dear Booth . . . and it's just as silly.

Edward   Suppose I tackle the job?

Alice   Not because I want you to?

Edward   Do you? No . . . you shan't have to think that.

Alice   But my dear . . . I shall be so proud of you.

Edward   When I've failed?

Alice   I shan't think it failure.

Edward   Booth and Hugh and the rest must hold their tongues. I needn't have told them.

Alice   They'll do that much for you.

Edward   But I rather liked telling them too.

She is looking at him with suddenly shining eyes.

Alice   Edward . . . I'm so happy. Suddenly . . . you're a different man.

Edward   Am I?

Alice   You've begun to be. It was in you to be . . . and I knew it.

His face darkens.

Edward   I wonder . . . I wonder if I'm not . . . already!

Alice   Why . . . ?

Edward   And if my father didn't begin . . . just like this? He told me he did. Doing the right thing in the wrong way . . . then doing the wrong thing . . . and coming to be what he was . . . and bringing me to this. Alice, suppose it's not failure I'm risking . . . but success. Yes, you're right . . . I feel a different man.

She brings him help.

Alice   I'll take that risk, my dear. I'll risk your turning crook. And it's a pretty big risk now for me.

He accepts it.

Edward   Then there's no more to be said, is there?

Alice   Not for the moment.

He does not ask what she means by this.

I must go back to Honor. Horrid . . . if one knew it to look comic when one is suffering. (*As she opens the door.*) And here's Booth back again.

Edward   Shall I tell him he has convinced me?

Alice (*mischievously*)   It would delight him. But I shouldn't.

Act Four

Mr Voysey's *room at the office is* **Edward**'s *room now. It has somehow lost that brilliancy which the old man's occupation seemed to give it. Perhaps it is only because this December morning is dull and depressing; but the fire isn't bright and the panels and windows don't shine as they did. There are no roses on the table either.* **Edward**, *walking in as his father did, hanging his hat and coat where his father's used to hang, is certainly the palest shadow of that other masterful presence. A depressed, drooping shadow, too. This may be what* **Peacey** *feels; for he looks very surly as he obeys the old routine of following his chief to this room on his arrival. Nor has* **Edward** *so much as a glance for his confidential clerk. They exchange the most formal of greetings.* **Edward** *sits at his desk, on which lies the morning's pile of letters, unopened now.*

Peacey Good morning, sir.

Edward Good morning, Peacey. Any notes for me?

Peacey Well, I've hardly been through the letters yet, sir.

Edward (*his eyebrows meeting*) Oh . . . and I'm late myself.

Peacey I'm very sorry, sir.

Edward If Mr Bullen calls, you had better show him those papers. Write to Metcalfe; say I've seen Mr Vickery this morning and that we hope for a decision from Mr Booth within a day or so. Better show me the letter.

Peacey Very good, sir.

Edward That's all, thank you.

Peacey *gets to the door, where he stops, looking not only surly but nervous now.*

Peacey May I speak to you a moment, sir?

Edward Certainly.

Peacey, *after a moment, makes an effort, purses his mouth and begins.*

Peacey   Bills are beginning to come in upon me as is usual at this season, sir. My son's allowance at Cambridge is now rather a heavy item of my expenditure. I hope that the custom of the firm isn't to be neglected now that you are the head of it, Mr Edward. Two hundred your father always made it at Christmas . . . in notes, if you please.

Towards the end of this **Edward** *begins to pay attention. When he answers his voice is harsh.*

Edward   Oh to be sure . . . your hush-money.

Peacey (*bridling*)   That's not a very pleasant word.

Edward   This is an unpleasant subject.

Peacey   Well, it's not one I wish to discuss. Mr Voysey would always give me the notes in an envelope when he shook hands with me at Christmas.

Edward   Notes I understand. But why not a rise in salary?

Peacey   Mr Voysey's custom, sir, from before my time. My father . . .

Edward   Yes. It's an hereditary pull you have over the firm, isn't it?

Peacey   When my father retired . . . he's been dead twenty-six years, Mr Edward . . . he simply said: 'I have told the governor you know what I know.' And Mr Voysey said: 'I treat you as I did your father, Peacey.' Never another word with him on the subject.

Edward   A very decent arrangement . . . and the thriftiest no doubt, of the raising of salaries there might have been no end.

Peacey   Mr Edward, that's uncalled for. We have served you and yours most faithfully. I know my father would sooner have cut off his hand than do anything to embarrass the firm.

Edward   But business is business, Peacey. Surely he could have had a partnership for the asking.

Peacey   That's another matter, sir.

Edward   Why?

Peacey   A matter of principle, if you'll excuse me. I must not be taken to approve of the firm's conduct. Nor did my dear father approve. And at anything like a partnership he would certainly have drawn the line.

Edward   My apologies.

Peacey   That's all right, sir. Always a bit of friction in coming to an understanding about anything, isn't there, sir?

He is going when **Edward**'*s question stops him.*

Edward   Why didn't you speak about this last Christmas?

Peacey   You were so upset about your father's death.

Edward   My father died the summer before that.

Peacey   Well . . . truthfully, Mr Edward?

Edward   As truthfully as you think suitable.

The irony of this is wasted on **Peacey**, *who becomes pleasantly candid.*

Peacey   Well, I'd always thought there must be a smash when your father died . . . but it didn't come. I couldn't make you out. So I thought I'd better keep quiet for a bit and say nothing.

Edward   I see. Your son's at Cambridge?

Peacey   Yes.

Edward   I wonder you didn't bring him into the firm.

Peacey (*taking this very kind*)   Thank you. But James will go to the bar. He'll have to wait his chance, of course. But he's a clever lad. And it's a good use for one's savings.

Edward   I feel sure he'll do well. I'm glad to have had this little talk with you, Peacey. I'm sorry you can't have the money.

He returns to his letters, a little steely-eyed. **Peacey** *quite at his ease, makes for the door yet again, saying . . .*

Peacey   Oh, any time will do, sir.

Edward   You can't have it at all.

Peacey (*brought up short*)   Can't I?

Edward   No. This was one of the first things I made up my mind about. The firm's business is not carried on quite as it used to be. You may have noticed that you don't get the same little matters passing through your hands. In fact, we no longer make illicit profits out of our clients. So there are none for you to share.

Peacey *bridles.*

Peacey   Mr Edward . . . I'm sorry we began this discussion. You'll give me my two hundred, please . . . and we'll drop the subject.

Edward   Yes . . . I've no more to say.

Peacey   I want the money. And it's hardly gentlemanly in you, Mr Edward, to try and get out of giving it me. Your father'd never have made such an excuse.

Edward   D'you think I'm lying to you?

Peacey   That is no business of mine, sir.

Edward   As long as the dividend is punctually paid.

Peacey   And there's no need to be sarcastic.

Edward   Would you rather I told you plainly what I think of you?

Peacey   That I'm a thief because I've taken money from a thief?

Edward   Worse! You're content to have others steal for you.

Peacey   And who isn't?

Edward *is really pleased with the retort. He relaxes and changes his tone, which had indeed become a little bullying.*

Edward   Ah, my dear Peacey . . . I fear we mustn't begin to talk economics. The present point is that I myself no longer receive these particular stolen goods. Therefore I can throw a stone at you. I have thrown it.

Peacey, *who would far sooner be bullied than talked to like this, turns very sulky indeed.*

Peacey   Then I resign my position here.

Edward   Very well.

Peacey   And I happen to think the secret's worth its price.

Edward   Perhaps someone will pay it you.

Peacey (*feebly threatening*)   Don't presume upon it's not being worth my while to make use of what I know.

Edward (*not unkindly*)   But, my good fellow, it happens to be the truth I'm telling you. I am doing a thankless . . . and an unpleasant . . . and a quite unprofitable job here. How can you hope to blackmail a man who has everything to gain by exposure and nothing to lose?

Peacey (*peevish*)   I don't want to ruin you, sir, and I have a great regard for the firm. But you must see that I can't have my income reduced in this way without a struggle.

Edward (*with great cheerfulness*)   Very well . . . struggle away.

Peacey (*his voice rising high and thin*)   But is it fair dealing on your part to dock the money suddenly like this ? I have been counting on it most of the year, and I have been led into heavy expenses. Why couldn't you have warned me?

Edward   Yes, that's true, Peacey . . . it was stupid of me. I'm sorry.

Peacey *is a little comforted by this quite candid acknowledgment.*

Peacey   Things may get easier for you by and by.

Edward   Possibly.

Peacey   Will you reconsider the matter then?

At this insinuation **Edward** *looks up, more than a little exasperated.*

Edward   Then you don't believe what I tell you?

Peacey   Yes, I do.

Edward   But you think that the fascination of swindling one's clients will finally prove irresistible?

Peacey   That's what your father found, I suppose you know.

This gives **Edward** *such pause that he drops his masterful tone.*

Edward   I didn't.

Peacey   He got things as right as rain once.

Edward   Did he?

Peacey   So my father told me. But he started again.

Edward   Are you sure of this?

Peacey (*expanding pleasantly*)   Well, sir, I knew your father pretty well. And when I first came into the firm I simply hated him. He was that sour . . . so snappy with everyone, as if he had a grievance against the whole world.

Edward (*pensively*)   He had, then . . . in those days!

Peacey   His dealings with his clients were no business of mine. I speak as I find. He came to be very kind to me . . . thoughtful and considerate. He was pleasant and generous to everyone . . .

Edward   So you have hopes of me yet?

Peacey (*who has a simple mind*)   No, Mr Edward, no. You're different from your father . . . one must make up one's mind to that. And you may believe me or not, but I should be very glad to know that the firm was going straight again. I'm getting on in years myself, now I'm not much longer for the business, and there've been times when I have sincerely regretted my connection with it. If you'll let me say so, I think it's very noble of you to have undertaken the work you have. (*Then, as everything seems smooth again.*) And if you'll give me enough to cover this year's extra expense, I think I may promise you that I shan't expect money again.

Edward (*good-tempered, as he would speak to an importunate child*) No, Peacey, no.

Peacey (*fretful again*)   Well, sir, you make things very difficult for me.

Edward   Here is a letter from Mr Cartwright which you might attend to. If he wants an appointment with me, don't make one till the New Year. His case can't come on before February.

Peacey (*taking the letter*)   I show myself anxious to meet you in every way . . . (*He is handed another.*)

Edward   'Perceval Building Estate' . . . that's yours too.

Peacey (*putting them both down, resolutely*)   But I refuse to be ignored. I must consider my whole position. I hope I may not be tempted to make use of the power I possess. But if I am driven to proceed to extremities . . .

Edward (*breaking in upon this bunch of tags*)   My dear Peacey, don't talk nonsense . . . you couldn't proceed to an extremity to save your life. You've comfortably taken this money all these years. You'll find you're no longer capable of doing even such a slightly uncomfortable thing as tripping up your neighbour.

This does completely upset the gentle blackmailer. He loses one grievance in another.

Peacey   Really, Mr Edward, I am a considerably older man than you. These personalities . . . !

Edward   I'm sorry. Don't forget the letters.

Peacey   I will not, sir.

He takes them with great dignity and is leaving the room.

There's Mr Hugh waiting.

Edward   To see me? Ask him in.

Peacey   Come in, Mr Hugh, please.

Hugh *comes in,* **Peacey** *holding the door for him with a frigid politeness of which he is quite oblivious. At this final slight* **Peacey** *goes out in dudgeon.*

Edward   How are you?

Hugh   I don't know.

And he throws himself into the chair by the fire. **Edward**, *quite used to this sort of thing, goes quietly on with his work, adding encouragingly after a moment . . .*

Edward   How's Beatrice?

Hugh   Ink to the elbows. She's halfway through her new book.

He studies his boots with the gloomiest expression. And, indeed, they are very dirty and his turned-up trousers are muddy at the edge. As he is quite capable of sitting silently by the fire for a whole morning **Edward** *asks him at last . . .*

Edward   Do you want anything?

Hugh   Yes . . . I want five bob. I left home without a penny. I've walked.

Edward   From Highgate?

Hugh   Yes . . . by Hornsey and Highbury and Hackney and Hoxton. And I must have some lunch.

Edward   I can manage five bob . . .

He puts them on his table.

Hugh   And Upper Holloway and Lower Holloway . . . and Pentonville . . . and Clerkenwell . . .

Edward   I don't know any of them.

Hugh   Nobody does . . . except the million people who live there. But that's London. And I also, my dear Edward, want it destroyed.

Edward   We are warned that . . . under certain circumstances . . . it may be.

Hugh   But why wait for mere foreigners to do the job? Not tackle it ourselves . . . and, in the inspiring words of Mr Rockefeller, d o it now?

Edward   And what about the people who live there?

Hugh   Why should they live there . . . or anywhere? Why should they live at all?

Edward   Well, they've their work to do . . . most of them. Incidentally . . . much as I love your society . . . so have I mine. And this morning I'm rather busy.

Hugh   Aha! There's the fatal word. We don't work, Edward, not one in a thousand of us. Work is creation. Is that what an outworn civilisation requires of us? Obviously not. It asks us to keep busy . . . and forget that to all these means there is no creative end at all. We've to keep our accounts straight . . . as you have to now . . . to keep the streets clean . . . and ourselves clean . . .

Edward   That at least may be called an end in itself.

Hugh   I'm not so sure. If it's merely a habit . . . all habits are bad habits. Why wash?

Edward   I seem to remember that, as a small boy, washing was not your strong point.

Hugh   I'm glad I had that much moral courage. On principle a man should not wash unless he feels an inward urge to wash. Did Michelangelo wash? Seldom!

Edward   Better his work than his company, then.

Hugh   I'm sick of this endless sham. But one can put some sort of an end to it . . . if not to all of it . . . to one's own small share in it. And I mean to. So that's that.

Edward   Suicide?

Hugh   Oh dear me no! Life's great fun if you could only live it. I mean to live it. Thanks for the five bob. (*He pockets it.*) And my first step is to hand you back for your wretched clients the money that the Pater settled on me . . . what there is left of it. And don't let me forget that I owe you this too.

Edward   But my dear Hugh, you can't afford . . .

Hugh   Aha! Another fatal word. Afford! Give a man an income . . . big or small . . . and he passes half his time thinking what he can or can't afford. The money has been a curse to me. It has never belonged to me.

Edward   No.

Hugh   Oh, never mind the legal . . . I mean in the r e a l sense. How could it belong to me? I didn't create it . . . or even earn it. I've belonged to it. So there's the first step to being free. My spiritual history is a very interesting one, Edward. If it weren't for Beatrice I'd make a book of it.

Edward   Would it show her up badly?

Hugh   No . . . but writing's h e r job. One mustn't poach.

Edward   She might make a book of it.

Hugh   Oh, it doesn't interest h e r. D'you remember the row there was at home when I said I meant to paint?

Edward   Very well.

Hugh   However . . . the Pater came down at last with two hundred a year. Studio rent, velvet coat, mutton chop cooked on the gas stove, and sardines for supper . . . that's what the art of painting meant to him. Then I got married to Beatrice . . . which was so unexpectedly moral of me that he sprang another two hundred. Well . . . I've kept busy. And I've learnt how to paint. And I do paint . . . other men's pictures.

Edward   Forgery?

Hugh   Yes . . . it is.

Edward   Are you joking?

Hugh   Not at all. Forty-nine out of fifty of us . . . if you put us to paint that table and chair . . . to begin with we don't s e e that table and chair! What we see is what we remember of some painting by Matisse or Picasso of some other table and chair. This world, my dear Edward, is growing fuller and fuller of paintings of paintings, and of paintings of paintings of paintings. And a couple of hundred of them must be mine, if I could afford it . . . aha, afford! . . . I'd buy them back and burn them. But the critics, dear Edward, much prefer paintings of paintings to paintings . . . for they know what to say about them. They rejoice when they see that bastard great-grandchild of Picasso's . . .

Edward's *table telephone rings.*

Edward Yes? Yes . . . in two minutes. I must turn you out, Hugh. What does Beatrice say, by the by?

Hugh About the money? Yes, there's that. I can't quite leave her with nothing.

Edward Are you leaving her?

Hugh We got married with the idea that we'd separate some time. And I can't be free unless I do.

Edward I thought you were so fond of each other.

Hugh I suppose in a sort of way we still are. We've always disagreed about everything. That used to be stimulating. But now when we argue we quarrel. And that's tiring.

Edward Do they know down at home that you're not getting on?

Hugh Emily may.

Edward For heaven's sake keep a good face on things for Christmas.

Hugh I don't believe I'll go down for Christmas.

Edward Nonsense! You can't hurt Mother's feelings by . . .

Hugh Do not expect me to pay homage to the Voysey family feelings. If we must have a hollow fraud to kow-tow before, there are many less brassy ones. Good Lord . . . you're not still taken in by them, surely . . . after the way we've all treated you? Even I've shirked asking you how you've been getting on here . . . for fear you'd start telling me. How are things, though?

Edward   I've not done so badly. Better than I thought I should, really! I've righted what I thought the four most scandalous cases . . . somewhat to the prejudice of the rest.

Hugh   Then can't you cut free?

Edward   And go to gaol?

Hugh (*really startled by this*)   But they won't . . .

Edward   But they will.

Hugh   And at any moment . . .

Edward   Yes. I live on the brink. For the first month or so I thought every knock at the door meant a push over it. But nothing happens. There are days . . . you wouldn't believe it . . . when I quite forget that I'm a criminal. And . . . it's possible . . . nothing may happen. And . . . at this moment . . . I really don't know whether I want it to or not.

Hugh   I should take the plunge.

Edward   Why?

Hugh   The longer you wait the worse it'll be for you, won't it?

Edward   Yes.

Hugh   The thing's telling on you too.

Edward   I know. My barber tries to sell me hair restorer.

Hugh   On your faculties. The damn thing is swallowing you up. Don't let it. You've no right to let your life be brought to nothing.

Edward   Does my life matter?

Hugh   But of course.

Edward (*the iron in his soul*)   That's where we differ. Still, now I've scavenged up the worst of the mess . . . and can only sit here drudging . . . improving things by thirty shillings here . . . and by seven pounds two and sixpence there . . . I do begin to understand Father a little better.

Hugh (*cheerfully*)   Oh . . . I'm all for the Pater. He played a great game. And what this civilisation needs . . . if we can't smash it up altogether . . . is a lot more men like him . . .

The door is opened and **Mr George Booth** *comes in. He looks older than he did and besides is evidently not in a happy frame of mind.*

Mr George Booth   Hello, Hugh. How are you, Edward?

Hugh   But what I'm going to do is to step out of my front door with five bob in my pocket. And I'll tramp . . . and I'll paint for my bread . . . the farmer . . . the farmer's wife or his dog or his cow . . . an honest bit of work done with dispatch for just what he thinks it's worth to him. And if I can earn my bread I'll know I'm some good . . . and if I can't I'll drown myself.

Edward   I should wait till the summer comes.

Hugh   I'll begin with your office boy. For two shillings I will do him a sketch of his spotty little countenance. Edward, may I propose it to him?

Edward   You may not. To begin with he can't afford two shillings.

Hugh   Aha! Afford! And of course he's very busy too?

Edward   If he isn't, I'll sack him.

Hugh   Good God . . . what a world! Goodbye.

He departs, not, we may be sure, to tramp the roads; but he has thoroughly enjoyed hearing himself talk.

Edward   Will you come here . . . or will you sit by the fire?

Mr George Booth   This'll do. I shan't keep you long.

Edward   Well . . . here's the Vickery correspondence. He will pay the extra rent, but . . .

Mr George Booth (*nervously*)   Yes . . . it isn't really that I've come about.

Edward   No?

Mr George Booth   Something less pleasant, I'm afraid.

Edward   Litigation? I trust not.

Mr George Booth   No . . . I'm getting too old to quarrel. No! I've made up my mind to withdraw my securities from the custody of your firm. I don't know what notice is usual.

He has got it out and feels better. **Edward** *has awaited such a shock for so long that now it has come he finds he feels nothing.*

Edward   To a good solicitor . . . five minutes. Ten for a poor one. Have you any particular reason for doing this, Mr Booth?

Mr George Booth (*thankful to be able to talk, and so he thinks, stave off reproaches*)   Oh . . . naturally . . . naturally! You can't but know, Edward, that I have never been able to feel that implicit confidence in you . . . in your abilities, your personality, that's to say . . which I reposed in your father. Well . . . hardly to be expected, was it?

Edward (*grimly acquiescent*)   Hardly.

Mr George Booth   It's nothing against you. Men like your father are few and far between. I don't doubt that things go on here as they have always done. But since he died, I have not been happy about my affairs. It is a new experience for me . . . to feel worried . . . especially about money. The possession of money has always been something of a pleasure to me. And my doctor . . . I saw him again yesterday . . . he keeps me on a diet now . . . quite unnecessary . . . but he said that above all things I was not to worry. And, as I made up my mind upon the matter some time ago . . . in point of fact more than a year before your father died, it was clear to me that I could not leave my interests in your hands as I had in his.

Edward (*this strikes him with the shock of a bullet*)   Did he know that?

Mr George Booth   He must have guessed. I practically told him so. And I hoped he'd tell you . . . and so spare me the unpleasant necessity of hurting your feelings . . . as I fear I must be doing now.

Edward   Not at all. But we'll take it, if you please, that he never guessed. (*For with that thought of his father he really could not live.*) I can't induce you to change your mind?

Mr George Booth   No. And I'd sooner you wouldn't try. I shall make a point of telling the family that you are in no way to blame. My idea is for the future to let my bank . . .

Edward   For it's my duty to, if I can . . .

Mr George Booth   Heavens above us, my dear Edward . . . the loss of one client . . . however important . . . !

Edward   I know. Well . . . here's the way out. And it isn't my fault.

Mr George Booth   Forgive me for saying that your conduct seems to me a little lacking in dignity.

Edward (*patient, ironic*)   I'm sure it must. Will you walk off with your papers now? They'll make rather a cart-load.

Mr George Booth   You'll have to explain matters a bit.

Edward (*grimly*)   Yes. I'd better. How much . . . Mr Booth . . . do you think you're worth?

Mr George Booth   God bless me . . . I k n o w what I'm worth. I'm not a baby . . . or a woman, I have it all written down . . . more or less . . . in a little book.

Edward   I should like to see that little book. You'll get not quite half of that out of us.

Mr George Booth   Don't be perverse, Edward. I said I had made up my mind to withdraw the whole . . .

Edward   You should have made it up sooner.

Mr George Booth   What's this all about?

Edward   The greater part of what is so neatly written down in that little book doesn't exist.

Mr George Booth   Nonsense. It must exist. I don't want to realise. You hand me over the securities. I don't need to reinvest simply because . . .

Edward (*dealing this blow not unkindly, but squarely*)   I can't hand you over what I haven't got.

The old man hears the words. But their meaning . . . ?

Mr George Booth   Is anything . . . wrong?

Edward   How many more times am I to tell you that we have robbed you of half your property?

Mr George Booth (*his senses almost failing him*)   Say that again.

Edward   It's quite true.

Mr George Booth   My money . . . gone?

Edward   Yes.

Mr George Booth (*clutching at a straw of anger*)   You've been the thief . . . you . . . you?

Edward   I wouldn't tell you so if I could help it . . . my father.

This actually calls **Mr Booth** *back to something like dignity and self-possession. He thumps* **Edward**'s *table furiously.*

Mr George Booth   I'll make you prove that.

Edward   Oh, you've fired a mine.

Mr George Booth (*scolding him well*)   Slandering your dead father, and lying to me . . . revenging yourself by frightening me . . . because I detest you!

Edward   Why . . . haven't I thanked you for pushing me over the edge? I do . . . I promise you I do.

Mr George Booth (*shouting; and his courage failing him as he shouts*)   Prove it . . . prove it to me. You don't frighten me so easily. One can't lose half of all one has and then be told of it in two minutes . . . sitting at a table. (*His voice tails off to a piteous whimper.*)

Edward (*quietly now and kindly*)   If my father had told you this in plain words, you'd have believed him.

Mr George Booth (*bowing his head*)   Yes.

Edward *looks at the poor old thing with great pity.*

Edward   What on earth did you want to do this for? You
need never have known . . . you could have died happy.
Settling with all those charities in your will would have smashed
us up. But proving your will is many years off yet, we'll hope.

Mr George Booth (*pathetic and bewildered*)   I don't understand.
No, I don't understand . . . because your father . . . ! But I
m u s t understand, Edward.

Edward   I shouldn't try to, if I were you. Pull yourself
together, Mr Booth. After all, this isn't a vital matter to you.
It's not even as if you had a family to consider . . . like some
of the others.

Mr George Booth (*vaguely*)   What others?

Edward   Don't imagine your money has been specially
selected for pilfering.

Mr George Booth (*with solemn incredulity*)   One has read of
this sort of thing. But I thought people always got found out.

Edward (*brutally humorous*)   Well . . . you've found us out.

Mr George Booth (*rising to the full appreciation of his wrongs*)
Oh . . . I've been foully cheated!

Edward (*patiently*)   Yes . . . I've told you so.

Mr George Booth (*his voice breaks, he appeals pitifully*)   But by
you, Edward . . . say it's by you.

Edward (*unable to resist his quiet revenge*)   I've not the ability or
the personality for such work, Mr Booth . . . nothing but the
remains of a few principles, which forbid me even to lie to you.

*The old gentleman draws a long breath and then speaks with great awe,
blending into grief.*

Mr George Booth   I think your father is in Hell. I loved
him, Edward . . . I loved him. How he could have had the
heart! We were friends for fifty years. And all he cared for was
to cheat me.

Edward (*venturing the comfort of an explanation*) No . . . he didn't value money quite as you do.

Mr George Booth (*with sudden shrill logic*) But he took it. What d'you mean by that?

Edward *leans back in his chair and changes the tenor of their talk.*

Edward Well, you are master of the situation now. What are you going to do?

Mr George Booth To get the money back?

Edward No, that's gone.

Mr George Booth Then give me what's left and –

Edward Are you going to prosecute?

Mr George Booth (*shifting uneasily in his chair*) Oh dear, is that necessary? Can't somebody else do that? I thought the law . . . ! What'll happen if I don't?

Edward What do you suppose I'm doing here now?

Mr George Booth (*as if he were being asked a riddle*) I don't know.

Edward (*earnestly*) When my father died, I began to try and put things straight. Then I made up my accounts . . . they can see who has lost and who hasn't and do as they please about it. And now I've set myself to a duller sort of work. I throw penny after penny hardly earned into the half-filled pit of our deficit. I've been doing that . . . for what it's worth . . . till this should happen. If you choose to let things alone . . . and hold your tongue . . . I can go on with the job till the next threat comes . . . and I'll beg that off too if I can. I've thought this my duty . . . and it's my duty to ask you to let me go on.

He searches **Mr Booth**'*s face and finds there only disbelief and fear. He bursts out.*

Oh you might at least believe me. It can't hurt you to believe me.

Mr George Booth   You must admit, Edward, it isn't easy to believe anything in this office . . . just for the moment,

Edward (*bowing to the extreme reasonableness of this*)   I suppose not. I can prove it to you. I'll take you through the books . . . you won't understand them . . . but I could prove it.

Mr George Booth   I think I'd rather not. Ought I to hold any further friendly communication with you now at all?

And at this he takes his hat.

Edward (*with a little explosion of contemptuous anger*)   Certainly not. Prosecute . . . prosecute!

Mr George Booth (*with dignity*)   Don't lose your temper. It's my place to be angry with you.

Edward   I shall be grateful if you'll prosecute.

Mr George Booth   It's all very puzzling, I suppose I must prosecute. I believe you're just trying to practise on my goodness of heart. Certainly I ought to prosecute. Oughtn't I? I suppose I must consult another solicitor.

Edward (*his chin in the air*)   Why not write to *The Times* about it?

Mr George Booth (*shocked and grieved at his attitude*)   Edward, how can you be so cool and heartless?

Edward (*changing his tone*)   D'you think I shan't be glad to sleep at night?

Mr George Booth   You may be put in prison.

Edward   I am in prison . . . a less pleasant one than Wormwood Scrubs. But we're all prisoners, Mr Booth.

Mr George Booth (*wagging his head*)   Yes. This is what comes of your free-thinking and philosophy. Why aren't you on your knees?

Edward   To you?

This was not what **Mr Booth** *meant, but he assumes a vicarious dignity of that sort.*

Mr George Booth   And why should you expect me to shrink from vindicating the law?

Edward (*shortly*)   I don't. I've explained you'll be doing me a kindness. When I'm wanted you'll find me here at my desk. (*Then as an afterthought.*) If you take long to decide, don't alter your behaviour to my family in the meantime. They know the main points of the business, and . . .

Mr George Booth (*knocked right off his balance*)   Do they? Good God! And I'm going there to dinner the day after tomorrow. It's Christmas Eve. The hypocrites!

Edward (*unmoved*)   I shall be there . . . that will have given you two days. Will you tell me then?

Mr George Booth (*protesting violently*)   But I can't go . . . I can't have dinner with them. I must be ill.

Edward (*with a half-smile*)   I remember I went to dine at Chislehurst to tell my father of my decision.

Mr George Booth (*testily*)   What decision?

Edward   To remain in the firm when I first learned what was happening.

Mr George Booth (*interested*)   Was I there?

Edward   I daresay.

Mr Booth *stands, hat, stick, gloves in hand, shaken by his experience, helpless, at his wits' end. He falls into a sort of fretful reverie, speaking half to himself, but yet as if he hoped that* **Edward**, *who is rapt in his own thoughts, would have the decency to answer, or at least listen to what he is saying.*

Mr George Booth   Yes, how often I dined with him! Oh, it was monstrous! (*His eyes fall on the clock.*) It's nearly lunchtime now. D'you know I can still hardly believe it all. I wish I hadn't found it out. If he hadn't died, I should never have found it out. I hate to have to be vindictive . . . it's not my nature. I'm sure I'm more grieved than angry. But it isn't as if it were a small sum. And I don't see that one is called upon to forgive crimes . . . or why does the law exist? This will go near to killing me. I'm too old to have such troubles. It isn't right. And if I have to prosecute . . .

Edward (*at last throwing in a word*)   Well . . . you need not.

Mr George Booth (*thankful for the provocation*)   Don't you attempt to influence me, sir. (*He turns to go.*)

Edward   And what's more . . . with the money you have left . . .

Edward *follows him politely.* **Mr Booth** *flings the door open.*

Mr George Booth   You'll make out a cheque for that at once, sir, and send it to me.

Edward   You might . . .

Mr George Booth (*clapping his hat on, stamping his stick*)   I shall do the right thing, sir . . . never fear.

So he marches off in fine style, he thinks, having had the last word and all. But **Edward**, *closing, the door after him, mutters . . .*

Edward   Save your soul . . . I'm afraid I was going to say.

Act Five

Naturally it is the dining room which bears the brunt of what an English household knows as Christmas decorations. They consist chiefly of the branches of holly, stuck cockeyed behind the top edges of the pictures. The one picture conspicuously not decorated is that which hangs over the fireplace, a portrait of **Mr Voysey**, *with its new gilt frame and its brass plate marking it also as a presentation. Otherwise the only difference between the dining room's appearance at half past nine on Christmas Eve and on any other evening in the year is that little piles of queer-shaped envelopes seem to be lying about, and quite a lot of tissue paper and string is to be seen peeping from odd corners. The electric light has been reduced to one bulb, but when the maid opens the door showing in* **Mr George Booth** *she switches on the rest.*

Mr George Booth   No, no . . . in here will do. Just tell Mr Edward.

Phoebe   Very well, sir.

She leaves him to fidget towards the fireplace and back, not removing his comforter or his coat, scarcely turning down the collar, screwing his cap in his hands. In a very short time **Edward** *comes in, shutting the door and taking stock of the visitor before he speaks.*

Edward   Well?

Mr George Booth (*feebly*)   I hope my excuse for not coming to dinner was acceptable. I did have . . . I have a very bad headache.

Edward   I daresay they believed it.

Mr George Booth   I have come at once to tell you my decision.

Edward   What is it?

Mr George Booth   I couldn't think the matter out alone. I went this afternoon to talk it over with the Vicar. After your father, he's my oldest friend now.

At this **Edward***'s eyebrows contract and then rise.*

Mr George Booth What a terrible shock to him!

Edward Oh, three of his four thousand pounds are quite safe.

Mr George Booth That you and your father . . . you, whom he baptised . . . should have robbed him! I never saw a man so utterly prostrate with grief. That it should have been your father! And his poor wife . . . though she never got on with your father.

Edward (*with cheerful irony*) Oh, Mrs Colpus knows too, does she?

Mr George Booth Of course he told Mrs Colpus. This is an unfortunate time for the storm to break on him. What with Christmas Day and Sunday following so close, they're as busy as can be. He has resolved that during this season of peace and goodwill he must put the matter from him if he can. But once Christmas is over . . . ! (*He envisages the old Vicar giving* **Edward** *a hell of a time then.*)

Edward (*coolly*) So you mean to prosecute. If you don't, you've inflicted on the Colpuses a lot of unnecessary pain and a certain amount of loss by telling them.

Mr George Booth (*naively*) I never thought of that. No, Edward, I have decided not to prosecute.

Edward *hides his face for a moment.*

Edward And I've been hoping to escape! Well, it can't be helped. (*And he sets his teeth.*)

Mr George Booth (*with touching solemnity*) I think I could not bear to see the family I have loved brought to such disgrace. And I want to ask your pardon Edward, for some of the hard thoughts I have had of you. I consider this effort of yours a very striking one. You devote all the firm's earnings, I gather, to restoring the misappropriated capital. Very proper.

Edward   Mr Booth . . . as I told you, you could help me . . . if you would. Your affairs, you see, are about the heaviest burden I carry.

Mr George Booth   Why is that?

Edward   My father naturally made freest with the funds of the people who trusted him most.

Mr George Booth   Naturally . . . you call it. Most unnatural, I think.

Edward (*finely*)   That also is true. And if you really want to help me, you could cut your losses . . . take interest only on the investments which do still exist . . .

Mr George Booth   No . . . forgive me. I have my own plan.

Edward   By prosecuting you'd be no better off . . .

Mr George Booth   Quite so. The very first thing the Vicar said. He has an excellent head for business. Of course his interests are small beside mine. But we stand together . . .

Edward *scents mischief and he looks straight at* **Mr Booth** . . . *very straight indeed.*

Edward   What is your plan?

Mr George Booth   Its moral basis . . . I quote the Vicar . . . is this. You admit, I take it, that there were degrees of moral turpitude in your father's conduct . . . that his treachery was blacker by far in some cases than in others.

Edward   I think I won't make that admission for the moment.

Mr George Booth   What . . . to cheat and betray a lifelong friend . . . and . . . and a man of God like the Vicar . . . is that no worse than a little ordinary trickiness? Now where are my notes? Our conditions are . . . one: we refrain from definitely undertaking not to prosecute . . . two: such securities as you have intact are to be returned to us at once . . .

Edward   Oh, certainly.

Mr George Booth   Three: the interest upon those others that have been made away with is to be paid.

Edward   As it has been so far.

Mr George Booth   We admit that. Four: the repayment of our lost capital is to be a first charge upon the . . . surplus earnings of the firm. There you are. And the Vicar and I both consider it very fair dealing.

Edward   D o you!

He goes off into peals of laughter.

Mr George Booth   Edward . . . don't laugh!

Edward   But it's very, very funny!

Mr George Booth   Stop laughing, Edward.

Edward   You refrain from undertaking n o t to prosecute . . . that's the neatest touch. That would keep me under your thumb, wouldn't it? (*Then with a sudden, savage snarl.*) Oh, you Christian gentlemen!

Mr George Booth   Don't be abusive, sir.

Edward   I'm giving my soul and body to restoring you and the rest of you to your precious money-bags. And you'll wring me dry . . . won't you? Won't you?

Mr George Booth   Don't be rhetorical. The money was ours . . . we want it back. That's reasonable.

Edward (*at the height of irony*)   Oh . . . most!

Mr George Booth   Any slight amendments to the plan . . . I'm willing to discuss them.

Edward (*as to a dog*)   Go to the devil.

Mr George Booth   And don't be rude.

Edward   I'm sorry.

There is a knock at the door.

Come in.

Honor *intrudes an apologetic head.*

Honor   Am I interrupting business?

Edward (*mirthlessly joking*)   No. Business is over . . . quite over. Come in, Honor.

Honor puts on the table a market basket bulging with little paper parcels, and, oblivious of **Mr Booth**'s *distracted face, tries to fix his attention.*

Honor   I thought, dear Mr Booth, perhaps you wouldn't mind carrying round this basket of things yourself. It's so very damp underfoot that I don't want to send one of the maids out tonight if I can possibly avoid it . . . and if one doesn't get Christmas presents the very first thing on Christmas morning quite half the pleasure in them is lost, don't you think?

Mr George Booth   Yes . . . yes.

Honor (*fishing out the parcels one by one*)   This is a bell for Mrs Williams . . . something she said she wanted so that you can ring for her, which saves the maids; cap and apron for Mary; cap and apron for Ellen; shawl for Davis when she goes out to the larder . . . all useful presents. And that's something for you . . . but you're not to look at it till the morning.

Having shaken each of them at the old gentleman, she proceeds to repack them. He is now trembling with anxiety to escape before any more of the family find him there.

Mr George Booth   Thank you . . . thank you. I hope my lot has arrived, I left instructions . . .

Honor   Quite safely . . . and I have hidden them. Presents are put on the breakfast table tomorrow.

Edward (*with an inconsequence that still, further alarms* **Mr Booth**) When we were children our Christmas breakfast was mostly made off chocolates.

Before the basket is packed, **Mrs Voysey** *sails slowly into the room as smiling and as deaf as ever.* **Mr Booth** *does his best not to scowl at her.*

Mrs Voysey   Are you feeling better, George Booth?

Mr George Booth   No. (*Then he elevates his voice with a shot of politeness.*) No, thank you . . . I can't say I am.

Mrs Voysey   You don't look better.

Mr George Booth   I still have my headache. (*With a distracted shout.*) Headache!

Mrs Voysey   Bilious, perhaps. I quite understand you didn't care to dine. But why not have taken your coat off? How foolish in this warm room!

Mr George Booth   Thank you. I'm . . . just going.

He seizes the market basket. At that moment **Beatrice** *appears.*

Beatrice   Your shawl, Mother. (*And she clasps it round* **Mrs Voysey**'s *shoulders.*)

Mrs Voysey   Thank you, Beatrice. I thought I had it on, (*Then to* **Mr Booth**, *who is now entangled in his comforter.*) A merry Christmas to you.

Beatrice   Good evening, Mr Booth.

Mr George Booth   I beg your pardon. Good evening, Mrs Hugh.

Honor (*with sudden inspiration, to the company in general*)   Why shouldn't I write in here . . . now the table's cleared?

Mr George Booth (*sternly, now he is safe by the door*)   Will you see me out, Edward?

Edward   Yes.

He follows the old man and his basket, leaving the others to distribute themselves about the room. It is a custom of the female members of the Voysey family, about Christmas time, to return to the dining room when the table has been cleared and occupy themselves in various ways which involve space and untidiness. **Beatrice** *has a little workbasket containing a buttonless glove and such things, which she is rectifying.* **Honor**'s *writing is done with the aid of an enormous blotting book, which bulges with apparently a year's correspondence. She sheds its contents upon the end of the dining table and spreads them abroad.* **Mrs Voysey** *settles to the* *table near to the fire, opens the* Nineteenth Century *and is instantly absorbed in it.*

Beatrice   If there's anywhere else left in this house where one can write or sew or sit, I'd be glad to know of it. Christmas tree in the back drawing room and all the furniture in the front! Presents piled up under dusters in the library! My heap is very soft and bulgy. Honor . . . if you've given me an eiderdown quilt I'll never forgive you.

Honor   Oh, I haven't . . . I shouldn't t h i n k of it.

Beatrice   And tomorrow this room will look like a six p.m. bargain counter.

Honor   But . . . Beatrice . . . it's Christmas.

Beatrice   Noël . . . Noël! Where's Emily?

Honor   Well . . . I'm afraid she's talking to Booth.

Beatrice   If you mean that Booth is listening to her, I don't believe it. She has taken my fine scissors.

Honor   And I think she's telling him about you.

Beatrice   What . . . in particular . . . about me?

Honor   About you and Hugh.

Beatrice   Now whose fault is this? We agreed that nothing more was to be said till after Christmas.

Honor   But Edward knows . . . and Mother knows

Beatrice   I warned Mother a year ago.

Honor   And Emily told me. And everyone seems to know except Booth. And it would be fearful if he found out. So I said: 'Tell him one night when he's in bed and very tired.' But Emily didn't seem to think that would . . .

At this moment **Emily** *comes in, looking rather trodden upon.* **Honor** *concludes in the most audible of whispers . . .*

Honor   Don't say anything . . . it's my fault.

Beatrice (*fixing her with a severe forefinger*)   Emily . . . have you taken my fine scissors?

Emily (*timidly*)   No, Beatrice.

Honor (*who is diving into the recesses of the blotting book*)   Oh, here they are! I must have taken them. I do apologise!

Emily (*more timidly still*)   I'm afraid Booth's rather cross. He's gone to look for Hugh.

Beatrice (*with a shake of her head*)   Honor . . . I've a good mind to make you do this sewing for me.

In comes the **Major**, *strepitant. He takes, so to speak, just enough time to train himself on* **Beatrice** *and then fires.*

Major Booth Voysey   Beatrice, what on earth is this Emily has been telling me?

Beatrice (*with elaborate calm*)   Emily, what have you been telling Booth?

Major Booth Voysey   Please . . . please do not prevaricate. Where is Hugh?

Mrs Voysey (*looking over her spectacles*)   What did you say, Booth?

Major Booth Voysey   I want Hugh, Mother.

Mrs Voysey   I thought you were playing billiards together.

Edward *strolls back from dispatching* **Mr Booth**, *his face thoughtful.*

Major Booth Voysey (*insistently*)   Edward, where is Hugh?

Edward (*with complete indifference*)   I don't know.

Major Booth Voysey (*in trumpet tones*)   Honor, will you oblige me by finding Hugh and saying I wish to speak to him here immediately.

Honor, *who has leapt at the sound of her name, flies from the room without a word.*

Beatrice   I know quite well what you want to talk about, Booth. Discuss the matter by all means if it amuses you . . . but don't shout.

Major Booth Voysey   I use the voice Nature has gifted me with, Beatrice.

Beatrice (*as she searches for a glove button*)   Nature did let herself go over your lungs.

Major Booth Voysey (*glaring round with indignation*)   This is a family matter . . . otherwise I should not feel it my duty to interfere . . . as I do. Any member of the family has a right to express an opinion. I want Mother's. Mother, what do you think?

Mrs Voysey (*amicably*)   What about?

Major Booth Voysey   Hugh and Beatrice separating.

Mrs Voysey   They haven't separated.

Major Booth Voysey   But they mean to.

Mrs Voysey   Fiddle-de-dee!

Major Booth Voysey   I quite agree with you.

Beatrice (*with a charming smile*)   Such reasoning would convert a stone.

Major Booth Voysey   Why have I not been told?

Beatrice   You have just been told.

Major Booth Voysey (*thunderously*)   Before.

Beatrice   The truth is, dear Booth, we're all so afraid of you.

Major Booth Voysey (*a little mollified*)   Ha . . . I should be glad to think that.

Beatrice (*sweetly*)   Don't you?

Major Booth Voysey (*intensely serious*)   Beatrice, your callousness shocks me. That you can dream of deserting Hugh . . . a man who, of all others, requires constant care and attention.

Beatrice   May I remark that the separation is as much Hugh's wish as mine?

Major Booth Voysey   I don't believe that.

Beatrice (*her eyebrows up*)   Really!

Major Booth Voysey   I don't imply that you're lying. But you must know that it's Hugh's nature to wish to do anything that he thinks anybody wishes him to do. All my life I've had to stand up for him . . . and, by Jove, I'll continue to do so.

Edward (*from the depths of his armchair*)   Booth . . . if you could manage to let this alone.

The door is flung almost off its hinges by **Hugh***, who then stands stamping and pale green with rage.*

Hugh   Look here, Booth . . . I will not have you interfering with my private affairs. Is one never to be free from your bullying?

Major Booth Voysey   You ought to be grateful.

Hugh   Well, I'm not.

Major Booth Voysey   This is a family affair.

Hugh   It is not!

Major Booth Voysey (at *the top of his voice*)   If all you can do is to contradict me . . . you'd better listen to what I've got to say . . . q u i e t l y.

Hugh*, quite shouted down, flings himself petulantly into a chair. A hushed pause.*

Emily (*in a still small voice*)   Would you like me to go, Booth?

Major Booth Voysey (*severely*)   No, Emily. Unless anything has been going on which cannot be discussed before you. (*More severely still.*) And I trust this is not so.

Beatrice   Nothing at all appropriate to that tone of voice has been . . . going on. We swear it.

Major Booth Voysey   Why do you wish to separate?

Hugh   What's the use of telling you? You won't understand.

Beatrice (*who sews on undisturbed*)   We don't get on well together.

Major Booth Voysey (*amazedly*)   Is that all?

Hugh (*snapping at him*)   Yes, that's all. Can you find a better reason?

Major Booth Voysey (*with brotherly contempt*)   I've given up expecting common sense from you. But Beatrice . . . ! (*His tone implores her to be reasonable.*)

Beatrice   Common sense is dry diet for the soul, you know.

Major Booth Voysey (*protesting*)   My dear girl . . . that sounds like a quotation from your latest book.

Beatrice   It isn't. I do think you might read that book . . . for the honour of the family.

Major Booth Voysey (*successfully sidetracked*)   I bought it at once, Beatrice, and . . .

Beatrice   That's the principal thing, of course.

Major Booth Voysey (*and discovering it*)   But do let us keep to the subject.

Beatrice (*with flattering sincerity*)   Certainly, Booth. And there is hardly any subject that I wouldn't ask your advice about. But upon this . . . please let me know better. Hugh and I will be happier apart.

Major Booth Voysey (*obstinately*)   Why?

Beatrice (*with resolute patience, having vented a little sigh*)   Hugh finds that my opinions distress him. And I have at last lost patience with Hugh.

Mrs Voysey (*who has been trying to follow this through her spectacles*) What does Beatrice say?

Major Booth Voysey (*translating into a loud sing-song*)   That she wishes to leave her husband because she has lost patience.

Mrs Voysey (*with considerable acrimony*)   Then you must be a very ill-tempered woman. Hugh has a sweet nature.

Hugh (*shouting self-consciously*)   Nonsense, Mother.

Beatrice (*shouting good humouredly*)   I quite agree with you, Mother. (*She continues to her husband in an even, just tone.*) You have a sweet nature, Hugh, and it is most difficult to get angry with you. I have been seven years working up to it. But now that I am angry I shall never get pleased again.

The **Major** *returns to his subject, refreshed by a moment's repose.*

Major Booth Voysey   How has he failed in his duty? Tell us. I'm not bigoted in his favour. I know your faults, Hugh.

He wags his head at **Hugh**, *who writhes with irritation.*

Hugh   Why can't you leave them alone . . . leave us alone?

Beatrice   I'd state my case against Hugh if I thought he'd retaliate.

Hugh (*desperately rounding on his brother*)   If I tell you, you won't understand. You understand nothing! Beatrice thinks I ought to prostitute my art to make money.

Major Booth Voysey (*glancing at his wife*)   Please don't use metaphors of that sort.

Beatrice (*reasonably*)   Yes, I think Hugh ought to earn more money.

Major Booth Voysey (*quite pleased to be getting along at last*)   Well, why doesn't he?

Hugh   I don't want money.

Major Booth Voysey   How can you not want money? As well say you don't want bread.

Beatrice (*as she breaks off her cotton*)   It's when one has known what it is to be a little short of both.

Now the **Major** *spreads himself and begins to be very wise; while* **Hugh**, *to whom this is more intolerable than all, can only clutch his hair.*

Major Booth Voysey   You know I never considered art a very good profession for you, Hugh. And you won't even stick to one department of it. It's a profession that gets people into very bad habits, I consider. Couldn't you take up something else? You could still do those woodcuts in your spare time to amuse yourself.

Hugh (*commenting on this with two deliberate shouts of simulated mirth*)   Ha! Ha!

Major Booth Voysey   Well, it wouldn't much matter if you didn't do them at all.

Hugh   True!

Mrs Voysey *leaves her armchair for her favourite station at the dining table.*

Mrs Voysey   Booth is the only one of you that I can hear at all distinctly. But if you two foolish young people think you want to separate . . . try it. You'll soon come back to each other and be glad to. People can't fight against nature for long. And marriage is a natural state . . . once you're married.

Major Booth Voysey (*with intense approval*)   Quite right, Mother.

Mrs Voysey   I know.

She resumes the Nineteenth Century. *And the* **Major**, *to the despair of everybody, makes yet another start, trying oratory this time.*

Major Booth Voysey   My own opinion is, Beatrice and Hugh, that you don't realise the meaning of the word marriage. I don't call myself a religious man . . . but, dash it all, you were married in church. And you then entered upon an awful compact . . . ! Surely, as a woman, Beatrice, the religious point of it ought to appeal to you. Good Lord . . . suppose everybody were to carry on like this! And have you considered that . . . whether you are right, or whether you are wrong . . . if you desert Hugh you cut yourself off from the family.

Beatrice (*with the sweetest of smiles*)   That will distress me terribly.

Major Booth Voysey (*not doubting her for a moment*)   Of course.

Hugh *flings up his head, and finds relief at last in many words.*

Hugh   I wish to God I'd ever been able to cut myself off from the family! Look at Trenchard!

Major Booth Voysey (*gobbling a little at this unexpected attack*) I do not forgive Trenchard for his quarrel with the Pater.

Hugh   He quarrelled because that was his best way of escape.

Major Booth Voysey   Escape from what?

Hugh   From tyranny . . . from hypocrisy . . . from boredom! . . . from his Happy English Home.

Beatrice (*kindly*)   Now, my dear . . . it's no use . . .

Major Booth Voysey (*attempting sarcasm*)   Speak so that Mother can hear you!

But **Hugh** *isn't to be stopped now.*

Hugh   Why are we all dull, cubbish, uneducated . . . hopelessly middle-class!

Major Booth Voysey (*taking this as very personal*)   Cubbish!

Beatrice   Middle-class! Hugh . . . do think what you're saying.

Hugh   U p p e r middle-class, then. Yes . . . and snobbish too! What happens to you when you're born into that estate? What happened to us, anyhow? We were fed . . . we were clothed . . . we were taught and trained . . . and we were made comfortable. And that was the watchword given us: comfort! You must work for a comfortable livelihood. You must practise a comfortable morality . . . and go to your parson for spiritual comfort . . . and he'll promise you everlasting comfort in heaven. Far better be born in a slum . . . with a drunkard for a father and a drab for a mother . . .

Major Booth Voysey   I never heard such lunacy.

Hugh   If you're nothing and nobody, you may find it in you to become something and somebody . . . and at least you learn what the world wants of you and what it doesn't. But do you think the world today couldn't do without u s? Strip yourself of your comfortable income . . . as Edward here told you to . . . and step out into the street and see.

Major Booth Voysey (*ponderously*)   I venture to think . . .

Hugh   Oh no, you don't. You don't do either . . . and you'd better not try . . . for a little thinking might tell you that we and our like have ceased to exist at all. Yes, I mean it. Trenchard escaped in time. You went into the Army . . . so how could you discover what a back number you are? But I found out soon enough . . . when I tried to express myself in art . . . that there was nothing to express except a few habits, and tags of other people's thoughts and feelings. There is no Me . . . that's what's the matter. I'm an illusion. Not that it does matter to anyone but me. And look at Honor . . .

Major Booth Voysey   Honor leads a useful life . . . and a happy one. We all love her.

Hugh   Yes . . . and what have we always called her? Mother's right hand! I wonder they bothered to give her a name. By the time little Ethel came they were tired of training children. She was alive . . . in a silly, innocent sort of way. And then . . .

Beatrice   Poor little Ethel!

Major Booth Voysey   Poor Ethel!

They speak as one speaks of the dead.

Hugh   And though your luck has been pretty poor, Edward, you've come up against realities at least . . . against something that could make a man of you. (*Then back to his humorous savagery.*) But if Booth thinks this world will stand still because he and his like want to be comfortable . . . that's where he's wrong.

Major Booth Voysey (*dignified and judicious*)   We will return, if you please, to the original subject of discussion. This question of a separation.

Hugh *jumps up, past all patience.*

Hugh   Beatrice and I mean to separate. And nothing you may say will prevent it. The only trouble is money. She says we must have enough to live apart comfortably.

Beatrice (*in kindly irony*)   Yes . . . comfortably!

Hugh   And I daresay she's right . . . she generally is. So the question is: Can we raise it?

Major Booth Voysey   Well?

Hugh   Well . . . for the moment we can't.

Major Booth Voysey   Well then?

Hugh   So we can't separate.

Major Booth Voysey   Then what in heaven's name have we been discussing it for?

Hugh   I haven't discussed it. I don't want to discuss it. Why can't you mind your own business? Now I'll go back to the billiard room and my book.

He is gone before the **Major** *can recover his breath.*

Major Booth Voysey   I am not an impatient man . . . but really . . . !

Beatrice   Hugh's tragedy is that he is just clever enough to have found himself out . . . and no cleverer.

Major Booth Voysey (*magnanimous but stern*)   I will be frank. You have never made the best of Hugh.

Beatrice   No . . . at the worst it never came to that.

Major Booth Voysey   I am glad . . . for both your sakes . . . that you can't separate.

Beatrice   As soon as I am earning enough I shall walk off from him.

The **Major**'s *manly spirit stirs.*

Major Booth Voysey   You will do nothing of the sort, Beatrice.

Beatrice (*unruffled*)   How will you stop me, Booth?

Major Booth Voysey   I shall tell Hugh he must command you to stay.

Beatrice (*with a little smile*)   I wonder, would that make the difference. It was one of the illusions of my girlhood that I'd love a man who would master me.

Major Booth Voysey   Hugh must assert himself

He begins to walk about, giving some indication of how it should be done. **Beatrice**'s *smile has vanished.*

Beatrice   Don't think I've enjoyed wearing the breeches . . . to use that horrid phrase . . . all through my married life. But someone had to plan and make decisions and do accounts. We weren't sparrows or lilies of the field . . : (*She becomes conscious of his strutting and smiles rather mischievously.*) Ah . . . if I'd married you, Booth!

Booth's *face grows beatific.*

Major Booth Voysey   Well, I own to thinking that I am a masterful man . . . that it's the duty of every man to be so. (*He adds forgivingly.*) Poor old Hugh!

Beatrice (*unable to resist temptation*)   If I'd tried to leave you, Booth, you'd have whipped me . . . wouldn't you?

Major Booth Voysey (*ecstatically complacent*)   Ha . . . well . . . !

Beatrice   Do say yes. Think how it will frighten Emily.

The **Major** *strokes his moustache and is most friendly.*

Major Booth Voysey   Hugh's been a worry to me all my life. And now . . . as head of the family . . . well, I suppose I'd better go and give the dear chap a quiet talking to. I see your point of view, Beatrice.

Beatrice   Why disturb him at his book?

The **Major** *leaves them, squaring his shoulders as becomes a lord of creation. The two sisters-in-law go on with their work silently for a moment; then* **Beatrice** *adds . . .*

Beatrice   Do you find Booth difficult to manage, Emily?

Emily (*putting down her knitting to consider the matter*)   No. It's best to let him talk himself out. When he has done that he'll often come to me for advice. But I like him to get his own way as much as possible . . . or think he's getting it. Otherwise he becomes so depressed.

Beatrice (*quietly amused*)   Edward shouldn't be listening to this. (*Then to him.*) Your presence profanes these Mysteries.

Edward   I won't tell . . . and I'm a bachelor.

Emily (*solemnly, as she takes up her knitting* again) Do you really mean to leave Hugh?

Beatrice (*slightly impatient*)   Emily, I've said so.

They are joined by **Alice Maitland**, *who comes in gaily.*

Alice   What's Booth shouting about in the billiard room?

Emily (*pained*)   Oh . . . on Christmas Eve, too!

Beatrice   Don't y o u take any interest in my matrimonial affairs?

Mrs Voysey *shuts up the* Nineteenth Century *and removes her spectacles.*

Mrs Voysey   That's a very interesting article. The Chinese Empire must be in a shocking state. Is it ten o'clock yet?

Edward   Past.

Mrs Voysey (*as* **Edward** *is behind her*)   Can anyone see the clock?

Alice   It's past ten, Auntie.

Mrs Voysey   Then I think I'll go to my room.

Emily   Shall I come and look after you, Mother?

Mrs Voysey   If you'd find Honor for me, Emily.

Emily *goes in search of the harmless, necessary* **Honor**, *and* **Mrs Voysey** *begins her nightly chant of departure.*

Mrs Voysey   Goodnight, Alice. Goodnight, Edward.

Edward   Goodnight, Mother.

Mrs Voysey (*with sudden severity*)   I'm not pleased with you, Beatrice.

Beatrice   I'm sorry, Mother.

But without waiting to be answered the old lady has sailed out of the room. **Beatrice**, **Edward** *and* **Alice**, *now left together, are attuned to each other enough to be able to talk with ease.*

Beatrice   But there's something in what Hugh says about this family. Had your great-grandfather a comfortable income, Edward?

Edward   I think so. It was his father made the money . . . in trade.

Beatrice   Which has been filtering away ever since. But fairly profitably, surely . . . to the rest of the world. You'd a great-aunt who was quite a botanist and an uncle who edited Catullus, hadn't you?

Edward   Yes.

She is beginning to work out his theme.

Beatrice   Well, that didn't pay them. Then there was the uncle killed in the Sudan. A captain's pension and no more wouldn't have been much for a widow and four children.

Alice   Five.

Beatrice   Was it? Dear me . . . how prolific we were! And though I chaff Booth . . . I've seen him with his regiment giving weedy young slackers chest and biceps and making them 'decent chaps'. It takes a few generations, you know, to breed men who'll feel that it pays to do that for its own sake . . . and

who'll be proud to do it. Oh, I can find a lot to say for the
Upper Middle Class.

Edward   The family's petering out as its income does. D'you
notice that? Six of us. But there are only Booth's two children.

Beatrice   It's more than the shrinking income that's doing it
. . . more even than Hugh's 'worship of comfort'. Some fresh
impulse to assert itself . . . I expect that is what a class needs to
keep it socially alive. Well . . . your father developed one.

Edward   Not a very happy one!

Beatrice   It might have been . . . if he'd had the good sense
to borrow the money for his financial operations just a little
less casually.

Edward   D'you know what I think I've found out about him
now?

Beatrice   Something interesting, I'm sure.

Edward   He did save my grandfather and the firm from a
smash. That was true. A pretty capable piece of heroism!
Then . . . six years after . . . he started on his own account
cheating again. I suppose he found himself in a corner . . .

Beatrice (*psychologically fascinated*)   Not a bit of it! He did it
deliberately. One day when he was feeling extra fit he must
have said to himself: 'Why not? . . . well, here goes!' You never
understood your father. I do . . . it's my business to.

Edward   He was an old scoundrel, Beatrice, and it's
sophistry to pretend otherwise.

Beatrice   But he was a bit of a genius too. You can't be
expected to appreciate that. It's tiresome work, I know . . .
tidying up after these little Napoleons. He really did make
money, didn't he, besides stealing it?

Edward   Lord, yes! And I daresay more than he stole. An
honest two thousand a year from the firm. He had another
thousand . . . and he spent about ten. He must have found the
difference somewhere.

Beatrice   There you are, then. And we all loved him. You did, too, Alice.

Alice   I adored him.

Edward   He was a scoundrel and a thief.

Alice   I always knew he was a scoundrel of some sort. I thought he probably had another family somewhere.

Beatrice   Oh . . . what fun! Had he, Edward?

Edward   I fancy not.

Beatrice   No, he wasn't that sort . . . and it spoils the picture to overcrowd it.

Edward   Pleasant to be able to sit back and survey the business so coolly.

Beatrice   Somebody has to . . . some time or other . . . try to find a meaning in this and everything that happens . . . or we should run mad under what seems the wicked folly of it all. But it's only the flippant and callous little bit of me which writes my flippant and callous little books that sits back so coolly, Edward. And even that bit . . . when you're not looking . . . stands up to make you a pretty low bow. Aren't matters any better . . . aren't you nearly through?

Edward   Yes, they are better.

Beatrice   I'm glad. Have you ever been sorry that you didn't do the obviously wise thing . . . uncover the crime and let the law take its course?

Edward   Often.

Beatrice   Why did you take up the challenge single-handed . . . lawlessly . . . now that perhaps you can look back and tell?

Edward *rather unwillingly, rather shyly, confesses.*

Edward   I think that I wanted . . . quite selfishly . . . a little vaingloriously, I daresay . . . to prove what my honesty was worth . . . what I was worth. And I was up against it. (*After*

which comes, perhaps, a more inward truth.) And then, you know,
I loved the Pater.

Beatrice (*touched*)   In spite of all?

Edward   Oh, yes. And I felt that if the worst of what he'd
recklessly done was put right . . . it might be the better for him
somehow.

Beatrice, *who has no such superstitious beliefs, lets this sink in on her
nevertheless.*

Beatrice   Silence in the Court.

Another moment, and she collects her sewing, gets up and goes. **Alice** *has
had all the while a keen eye on* **Edward**.

Alice   But something has happened since dinner.

Edward   Could you see that?

Alice   Tell me.

Edward (*as one throwing off a burden*)   The smash has come . . .
and it's not my fault. Old George Booth . . .

Alice   I knew he'd been here.

Edward   He found out . . . I had to tell him. You can
imagine him. I told him to take what was left of his money
and prosecute. Well . . . he'll take what he can get and he
won't prosecute. For he wants to bleed me, sovereign by
sovereign as I earn sovereign by sovereign, till he has got the
rest. And he has told the Vicar . . . who has told his wife . . .
who has told the choirboys by this time I daresay. So it's a
smash. And I thank God for it.

Alice (*quiet but intent*)   And what'll happen now?

Edward   One can't be sure. Gaol, possibly. I'll be struck off
the Rolls anyhow. No more Lincoln's Inn for me.

Alice   And what then?

Edward   I don't know . . . and I don't care.

Alice (*still quieter*)   But I do.

Edward   Oh, I shan't shoot myself. I've never cared enough about my life to take the trouble to end it. But I'm damned tired, Alice. I think I could sleep for a week. I hope they won't undo what I've done, though. They won't find it very easy to . . . that's one thing. And I shan't help them. Well, there it is. Nobody else knows yet. I like you to be the first to know. That's all. A merry Christmas. Goodnight.

As he takes no more notice of her, **Alice** *gets up and goes to the door. There she pauses, and turns; and then she comes back to him.*

Alice   I'm supposed to be off to Egypt on the twenty-eighth for three months. No, I'm not ill. But, as I've never yet had anything to do except look after myself, the doctor thinks Egypt might be . . . most beneficial.

Edward   Well, you may find me still at large when you come back.

Alice   Oh, I'm not going . . . now.

Edward (*sharply*)   Why not? Good God . . . don't make it worse for me. To have you about while I'm being put through this . . . have you reading the reports the next morning . . . coming into court perhaps to look pityingly at me! Go away . . . and stay away. That's all I ask.

Alice (*unperturbed*)   At the best, I suppose, you'll be left pretty hard up for the time being.

Edward   If His Majesty doesn't find me a new suit, they'll leave me the clothes on my back.

Alice   What a good thing I've my eight hundred a year!

Edward (*with a gasp and a swallow*)   And what exactly do you mean by that?

Alice   Could they take my money as well . . . if we were married already? I've never been clear about married women's property. But you know. It's your business to. Could they?

Edward (*choking now*)   Are you . . . are you . . . ?

Alice   Because if they could it would be only sensible to wait a little. But if not . . .

Edward *hardens himself.*

Edward   Look here, now. Through these two damnable years there's only one thing I've been thanking God for . . . that you never did say yes to me,

Alice (*chaffing him tenderly*)   Four times and a half you proposed. The first time on a walk we took down in Devon . . . when you cut a stick of willow and showed me how to make a whistle from it. I have that still . . . and there are four and a half notches in it. The half was only a hint you dropped. But I could have caught you on it if I'd wanted to.

Edward   Well . . . you didn't.

Alice   No. But I kept the stick.

Edward   If you didn't care enough for me to marry me then . . .

Alice   Well . . . I didn't.

Edward   You don't suppose that now your eight hundred a year . . .

Alice   Are you still in love with me, Edward?

Edward *sets his teeth against temptation.*

Edward   The answer must be no.

She smiles.

Alice   You're lying.

Edward   Can't we stop this? I've had about as much as I can stand.

Alice   Don't be so difficult. If I ask you to marry me, you'll refuse. And then what can I do? I can't coquette and be alluring. I don't know how.

Edward (*trying to joke his way out*)   Something to be thankful for!

Alice   But, my dear . . . I love you. I didn't before. I thought you were only a well-principled prig. I was wrong. You're a man . . . and I love you with all my heart and soul. Oh . . . please . . . please ask me to be your wife.

Edward (*for he resists happiness no more*) If I've luck . . . if they let me go free . . .

Alice   No . . . now . . . now . . . while you're in trouble. I won't take you later . . . when the worst is over. I'm dashed if I do. I'll marry you tomorrow.

Edward (*objecting but helplessly*)   That's Christmas Day.

Alice   And Boxing Day's next. Well, the old wretch of a Vicar can marry us on Saturday.

Edward (*giving his conscience one more hysterical chance*)   I haven't asked you yet.

Alice   I don't believe, you know, that they will put you in prison. It would be so extraordinarily senseless.

Edward   But now the scandal's out, we must go smash in any case.

Alice   You couldn't call them all together . . . get them round a table and explain? They won't all be like Mr Booth and the Vicar. Couldn't we bargain with them to let us go on?

The 'we' and the 'us' come naturally.

Edward   But . . . heavens above . . . I don't want to go on. You don't know what the life has been.

Alice   Yes, I do. I see when I look at you. But it was partly the fear, wasn't it . . . or the hope . . . that this would happen. Once it's all open and above-board . . . ! Besides you've had no other life. Now there's to be ours. That'll make a difference.

Edward (*considering the matter*)   They just might agree . . . to syndicate themselves . . . and to keep me slaving at it.

Alice   You could make them.

Edward   I! I believe my father could have . . . if that way out had taken his fancy.

Alice (*her pride in him surging up*)   My dear . . . don't you know yourself yet . . . as I now know you, thank God? You're ten times the man he ever was. What was he after all but a fraud?

Edward (*soberly*)   Well . . . I'll try.

Alice (*gentle and grave*)   I'm sure you should.

For a moment they sit quietly there, thinking of the future, uncertain of everything but one thing.

The others must have gone up to bed. This is no way for an Upper Middle-Class Lady to behave . . . sitting up hob-nobbing with you. Goodnight.

Edward   Goodnight. God bless you.

She is going again, but again she stops, and says half-humorously.

Alice   But even now you haven't asked me.

Edward (*simply*)   Will you marry me?

Alice (*as simply in return*)   Yes. Yes, please. (*Then, moving nearer to him.*) Kiss me.

Edward (*half-humorously too*)   I was going to.

And he does, with a passion that has reverence in it too.

Alice   Oh, my dear, my very dear. Till tomorrow then.

Edward   Till tomorrow.

She leaves him sitting there; a man conscious of new strength.